D1560643

Identity Attack Vectors

Implementing an Effective Identity and Access Management Solution

Morey J. Haber
Darran Rolls

Apress®

Identity Attack Vectors: Implementing an Effective Identity and Access Management Solution

Morey J. Haber
ORLANDO, FL, USA

Darran Rolls
AUSTIN, TX, USA

ISBN-13 (pbk): 978-1-4842-5164-5
https://doi.org/10.1007/978-1-4842-5165-2

ISBN-13 (electronic): 978-1-4842-5165-2

Managing Director, Apress Media LLC: Welmoed Spahr
Acquisitions Editor: Susan McDermott
Development Editor: Laura Berendson
Coordinating Editor: Rita Fernando

Cover designed by eStudioCalamar

Cover image designed by Freepik (www.freepik.com)

Distributed to the book trade worldwide by Springer Science+Business Media New York, 233 Spring Street, 6th Floor, New York, NY 10013. Phone 1-800-SPRINGER, fax (201) 348-4505, e-mail orders-ny@springer-sbm.com, or visit www.springeronline.com. Apress Media, LLC is a California LLC and the sole member (owner) is Springer Science + Business Media Finance Inc (SSBM Finance Inc). SSBM Finance Inc is a **Delaware** corporation.

For information on translations, please e-mail rights@apress.com, or visit http://www.apress.com/rights-permissions.

Apress titles may be purchased in bulk for academic, corporate, or promotional use. eBook versions and licenses are also available for most titles. For more information, reference our Print and eBook Bulk Sales web page at http://www.apress.com/bulk-sales.

Any source code or other supplementary material referenced by the author in this book is available to readers on GitHub via the book's product page, located at www.apress.com/9781484251645. For more detailed information, please visit http://www.apress.com/source-code.

Printed on acid-free paper

We would like to dedicate this book to no one in particular, because if we did, you would know their identity.

Table of Contents

About the Authors

Morey J. **Haber** is Chief Technology Officer and Chief Information Security Officer at BeyondTrust. He has more than 20 years of IT industry experience and has authored two Apress books: *Privileged Attack Vectors* and *Asset Attack Vectors*. In 2018, Bomgar acquired BeyondTrust and retained the BeyondTrust name. He originally joined BeyondTrust in 2012 as a part of the eEye Digital Security acquisition. Morey currently oversees BeyondTrust strategy for privileged access management (PAM), remote access, and vulnerability management (VM) solutions. In 2004, he joined eEye as Director of Security Engineering and was responsible for strategic business discussions and vulnerability management architectures in Fortune 500 clients. Prior to eEye, he was Development Manager for Computer Associates, Inc. (CA), responsible for new product beta cycles and named customer accounts. He began his career as Reliability and Maintainability Engineer for a government contractor building flight and training simulators. He earned a Bachelor of Science degree in Electrical Engineering from the State University of New York at Stony Brook.

Darran Rolls is CISO and Chief Technology Officer at SailPoint, where he is responsible for directing the company's technology strategy and security operations. He has a long history in identity management and security at companies such as Tivoli Systems, IBM, Waveset Technologies, and Sun Microsystems. He has helped design, build, and deliver innovative, groundbreaking technology solutions that have defined and shaped the identity and access management (IAM) industry. Over the last 25 years he has been a regular speaker at identity & security industry events worldwide and is a respected expert in the field of security, privacy, governance and administration for identity. Darran is a regular contributor to industry standards efforts and continues to help drive the adoption of standardization in and around identity and access management.

About the Technical Reviewer

Derek A. Smith is an expert at cybersecurity, cyber forensics, healthcare IT, SCADA security, physical security, investigations, organizational leadership, and training. He is currently an IT supervisor within the federal government and a cybersecurity associate professor at the University of Maryland, University College, and the Virginia University of Science and Technology and runs a small cybersecurity training company as well as a private investigations firm concentrating on digital forensics. Derek has completed four cybersecurity books and contributed a chapter for a fourth. He currently speaks at cybersecurity events throughout America and performs webinars for several companies as one of their cyber experts. Formerly, Derek worked for a number of IT companies, Computer Sciences Corporation and Booz Allen Hamilton among them. Derek spent 18 years as a special agent for various government agencies and the military. He has also taught business and IT courses at several universities for over 25 years. Derek has served in the US Navy, Air Force, and Army for a total of 24 years. He completed a doctorate degree in Organizational Leadership, an MBA, MS in IT Information Assurance, master's in IT Project Management, MS in Digital Forensics, BS in Education, and several associate degrees. He is currently enrolled in law school to obtain his Executive Juris Doctorate degree.

Acknowledgments

A very special thank you to the following for their contributions:

Matt Miller, Contributing Editor, Senior Content Marketing Manager, BeyondTrust
"Today, a picture is widely estimated to be worth a thousand words – this is reportedly down from ten thousand words when the equation was first introduced in the 1920s; with a ten-fold increase in the value of words in relation to pictures over the past 100 years, I'm betting heavily on the future for words."

Angela Duggan, Illustrations, Director of User Experience, BeyondTrust
"I believe good user experience isn't about being flashy or drawing attention; it should be seamless and go unnoticed. It is simply what people expect."

Neil McGlennon, Contributing Editor, Principal Technologiest Client & Partner Services, SailPoint Technologies.
"With knowledge as your compass, and practical application as your wind, you'll fare well through any seas."

Foreword

Consider this for a moment – no one at Amazon has ever physically seen me, verified my account information, or validated my signature. To Amazon, I am nothing but a bunch of various characters that, conveniently for me, make up my email address. As far as they are concerned, I don't have blue eyes or salt and pepper hair or any type of physically identifying characteristics. In fact, one could argue that I have no physical manifestation at all in their eyes.

Yet, Amazon knows my interests, likes, and dislikes probably better than anyone in the physical world. They know when to ship my workout drink so it arrives just in time and understand what book I want to read or video I want to watch next, all based on some random set of characters I chose over a decade ago.

And Amazon has the same perspective about hundreds of millions of users.

Of course, Amazon is not alone. Whether it is Google, Facebook, Netflix, or Twitter, this random collection of characters that is my email has become my online persona, my identity across unrelated platforms throughout the Internet. While this thought alone may be enough to give pause, the more concerning aspect is how this same model has become the foundation for identity management throughout the enterprise.

In a perimeter-less world, where anyone can access anything from anywhere, the first, and possibly only, line of defense we have is the Identity – that trusted moniker that validates access rights across the entire enterprise and provides a trustworthy foundation for risk-based decisions. Regrettably, most organizations never look past the "account" stage of an Identity, missing a major opportunity to develop an evolutionary program on which they can build their future program.

Unfortunately, in today's typical enterprise, an employee's email address has become the de facto standard way to identify users throughout the organization. Long gone are the days of esoteric, randomly generated usernames, which not only had little association with the person's actual name but typically had no meaningful context in any other system. For many valid reasons around user experience, technology has evolved to support a simpler, common mixed-mode identifier we know as our email address. By using this easy-to-remember moniker, infrastructure teams can leverage a single directory for the majority of authentication requests across the enterprise.

Sadly, while email addresses are easy for the user to remember, they are also widely publicized and shared on business cards, social media posts, and obviously, emails. Somehow, we've devolved to trusting the most public piece of information our users have and making authentication and authorization decisions based on it.

So, after those considerations, one must wonder why, as a security industry, we spend so much effort on protecting networks and servers and comparatively so little attention on understanding and protecting our users' identities. For decades, we have poured countless billions of dollars into perimeter protection, and yet, year over year, the number and severity of breaches continue to rise. Each year brings new attack vectors that we need to guard against, but yet, the goal of the attacks is usually the same: obtain account credentials, elevate the privileges of those accounts, and steal as much information as possible. Criminals need access to steal information and, without access credentials, that's nearly impossible.

As such, user identities are arguably the hottest commodity on today's underground market. Privileged access to devices, "critical" employee accounts, or shared identity information is sold and traded each day on the black market as the criminals move more toward persistent, deep access to an organization's infrastructure. While there will always be a section of the criminal element that is hell-bent on turning a quick buck with ransomware and the like, nation-state actors and more advanced adversaries are far more interested in the longer-term plays, that is, deep, persistent access to environments.

If we take a step back and look at what we do as security professionals, it is almost always based on an identity. Do we know who that network connection is from? Can we verify who's logged in to the application? Is the person who is sending a confidential email authorized to do so – and is the intended recipient authorized to receive it? Everything, in some way, is based on how we associate an action to a person. It doesn't matter what alert triggered or what vulnerability exists – the first question is almost always...Who?

With the network perimeter continuing its dissolution, and an almost obsessive move to cloud-based services, the user's identity is one of the last bastions of control still in the hands of enterprises. The ability to manage, monitor, and control user identities is a critical piece of functionality that must be in place in even the most basic environments. Sadly, that's much easier said than done. Identity Management projects are notoriously drawn out, disruptive, and, oftentimes, ill-fated.

Unlike many other security projects, an Identity Management project typically breaks down almost every technology/business barrier within an organization. One of the biggest challenges many Identity Management projects face is the integration of business applications with user directories that are deep in the infrastructure, frequently trying to connect modern UI services with outdated legacy directories. User roles (RBAC) and Separation of Duty (SoD) needs add layer after layer of complexity to the integration efforts, requiring an understanding of not just the technologies but of the business practices dependent on them as well.

In this latest addition to the "Attack Vectors" book series, Morey and Darran will help you navigate the complexities of managing identities throughout your enterprise. They provide some well-vetted practices of how to get your Identity Management program up and running, battle-tested advice on pitfalls to watch out for, and proactive methods to ensure long-term viability on your identity management program.

—John Masserini, CISO (`https://johnmasserini.com`)

Introduction

My name is Morey J. Haber. I am one of the authors of this book. My peer, Darran Rolls (the other author of this book), equally has his own name, and our names are a foundation reference for our identities. For me, it was given to me by my parents at birth and is an important concept for my own identity management. My name can change, or be changed, but my identity will always remain the same. It is a non-refutable fact.

However, I do have an alias identity – his name is John Titor. Just to set the record straight, I am not John Titor, nor do I know who he is or if he really exists. This is an alias bestowed upon me on the Internet by conspiracy theorists, "fact finders," and fanatics. It also represents the most bizarre case of identity impersonations and accusations I have seen in my 25+ years' career as a security and information technology professional.

For those of you who are not aware, John Titor is an identity used on several Internet bulletin boards during 2000 and 2001 by a person claiming to be an American military time traveler from the year 2036. John claims to have explicit knowledge of the future including specific predictions regarding catastrophic events in 2004 and a worldwide nuclear war which never came true. Internet readers latched on to the stories and where insistent to determine the truth behind the posts and outrageous claims. Some believed John to be a hoax perpetrated by myself, while others believe he really exists and is a time traveler with a secret mission. Unfortunately, multiple conspiracy theorists and hoax hunters have determined that my older brother Larry and I are the sources of the fiction and have repeatedly chastised us for creating it. To be fair, neither is true but freedom of speech allows these self-proclaimed journalists and investigators to brand me with original penmanship and the haunting of never-ending identity theft. As a public figure quoted in the press (that is what YouTube and Twitter have classified me as) and author of multiple books, social media providers will not censor these posts since it is the creator's opinion. If you need proof, just search the Internet for John Titor. The results may surprise you including posts, videos, and even a song or two.

John Titor however is not the subject of this book, but rather a muse for its creation. The story itself has been tied to my family name, my brothers, and fake news (well before #fakenews had its own hashtag) that have drawn incredibly questionable conclusions. Despite attempts to contact various accusers of my fake identity and explain the truth (what little I know of it), it will be forever branded as my alias. To that end, my family finds humor in this insanity even if, at times, it is annoying and intrusive, and social media blows up with allegations of my alias' fake identity. It is a never-ending battle to prove it is not true. If you ever need proof that the Internet has all sorts of hoaxes, search for information on a "tree octopus." If you haven't, I strongly recommend you put down this book and open your favorite Internet browser and begin searching for it.

Back yet? If that does not convince you enough that the Internet is full of fiction, aliases, and bogus identities, just start reading about John Titor as well and all your questions will be answered (sarcastically). And, if you add all the identity information on the Dark Web, the entire premise becomes even that much more confusing, for everyone.

To that end, my name is Morey J. Haber and my identity has been stolen (linked) by threat actors on the Internet who claim I am John Titor. I cannot change who I am. The linkage of my identity to this alias cannot be broken, and there are people who insist that it is true. This is an extreme, and absurd, case of identity theft. The attack vectors that it created are undeniably intense and clouded in the lore of the World Wide Web itself.

While I have incurred no discernable financial harm from this identity theft, some might question my tolerance for its annoyance. Other potential ramifications due to this threat could include legal, copyright, and travel inconveniences internationally or even government security clearance if this ever got out of control. After all these years, there is still no cure for many types of identity theft that myself and many others experience. The damages continue piling up and will be recurring for decades. This is why protecting everyone from identity theft and the attack vectors that can be used to own one's identity should be at the forefront of every security professional's mind.

And, if this type of attack can occur in someone's private life, imagine the threats if your identity was compromised in your professional life. The results could be devastating - not only to you, but to your organization as well.

To that end, once an identity is compromised, there is almost nothing than can be done to unwind all the fallout. All you can do is recover, solicit help, change passwords, and make amends wherever possible through resources compromised by your identity theft. It is a startlingly hard truth for too many people.

Even though this forward is personal in nature, this book centers around how an identity can be attacked, misused, misrepresented, and ultimately compromised in the business world. It will explore the concept of electronic identities and how to correctly set them up, philosophies for management, and how to protect them from identity theft and abuse. You will also learn the nuanced distinctions between identities, accounts, and credentials and how the relationship can be leveraged to attack privileges and assets. All of these fall under the Identity Governance (IG) umbrella and are often referred to as Identity Access Management (IAM).

Finally, we will cover the best practice steps and maturity model required for implementing an IAM solution within a corporate environment to minimize the risks of identity theft, manage identities, and adhere to regulatory compliance requirements that mandate Identity Governance.

While my personal issues with John Titor have now been laid bare, it is time to draw your attention to how this type of risk, by a threat actor, can damage you, your business, and your employees.

Identity theft is a serious crime and the attack vectors are complex. If we understand what an identity truly is, and what identity theft can really do, we can build effective defensive strategies to mitigate the potential threats.

CHAPTER 1

The Three Pillars of Cybersecurity

The foundation of cybersecurity defense has been muddied by point solutions, false promises, and "bolt-on" solutions that extend the value of a given technology based on a specific need. After all, if we each count the number of security solutions we have implemented, from antivirus and firewalls to security monitoring and single sign-on solutions, we will typically find dozens of vendors and hundreds of individual solutions throughout an organization. The average user or executive is not aware of most of the cybersecurity technology stack they depend upon, even though they may interact with most of it on a daily basis.

If we step back and try to group all of these solutions at a macro level, we will find each one falling into one of three logical groups. This is illustrated in Figure 1-1, the three pillars of cybersecurity.

© Morey J. Haber, Darran Rolls 2020
M. J. Haber and D. Rolls, *Identity Attack Vectors*, https://doi.org/10.1007/978-1-4842-5165-2_1

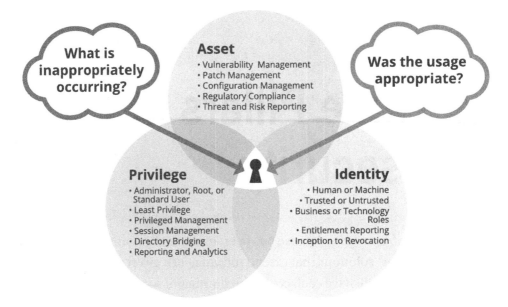

Figure 1-1. *The three pillars of cybersecurity*

These pillars can be described as

- **Identity** – The protection of a user's identity, account, and credentials from inappropriate access

- **Privilege** – The protection of the rights, privileges, and access control for an identity or account

- **Asset** – The protection of a resource used by an identity, directly or as a service

Although some solutions may be supersets of all three pillars, their goal is to unify information from each pillar in some form of correlation or analytics. Take, for example, a security information and event manager (SIEM) solution. It is designed to imbibe security data from solutions that reside in each group and then correlate the data to inform advanced threat detection and adaptive response. Correlation of common traits across the pillars enables a more holistic view of the environment. Time and date parameters are a typically connection point in most SIEM solutions. In others, connections between assets or identities provide a simplistic way of looking at how the pillars come together to support the entire cybersecurity foundation of your company. Let's look at a simple correlation:

- Who is this user (Identity)?

- What do they have access to (Privilege)?

- What did they access (Asset)?

- Is that access secured (Privilege)?

- Is that asset secured (Asset)?

- Was the access in accordance with the user's responsibilities (Identity)?

This helps answer the key question "What is **inappropriately** happening across my environment that I should be concerned about?" Answering this question is the primary goal of every security team and forms the basis for any incident management process. A good security program should provide coverage across all three pillars and identify solutions that provide meaningful data to help correlate across the boundaries of this overlapping Venn diagram.

Having this level of oversight and control helps answer the following questions:

- Are my assets and data secured?

- Are the privileges configured appropriately?

- Was the access by the right identity at the right time?

For most security vendors and their customers, the integration of these three pillars is critically important. If security solutions are isolated and do not share information, or only operate in their own silo, or between only two of the pillars, their detection and protection capabilities and data they can report will be limited in scope. For example, if an advanced threat protection solution or antivirus technology cannot share user information, or report on the context of the identity, then it is like riding a unicycle. The balance of information from the threat is not equally distributed. When processing threat information as an isolated log, event, or alert entry, key insights are missed. You need to have integrated data from all three pillars to be truly effective at dealing with modern threats.

If the unicycle analogy does not resonate with you, imagine not tracking privileged access to sensitive assets. You would never know if an identity is inappropriately accessing sensitive data. Moreover, you would never know if a compromised account is accessing sensitive data on what assets. Exploiting this lack of visibility is how threat actors are breaching our environments today. Without this visibility, we cannot track indicators of compromise and relate them back to the three pillars.

Therefore, when you look at new security or information technology solutions, ask yourself what pillar they occupy and how they can support the other pillars you trust and rely on every day. If they must operate in a single silo, make sure you understand why and what their relevance will be in the future. To this point, what is an example of a security solution that operates only in one silo? Answer – one that does not support any integrations nor operate between the three pillars. In many new deployments, this may sound like an Internet of Things (IoT) device or a traditional antivirus solution that can report on an infection on an asset but has no knowledge of the identity (account or user) or the privileges that the malware tried to use to infect the asset.

To that end, an IoT door lock or camera that provides physical protection for assets based on a static identity that cannot share access logs or integrate with current identity solutions is a bad choice for any organization. A standalone antivirus solution that has no central reporting on status, signature updates, or faults is another poor choice. There is no way of knowing if the AV is operating correctly, whether or not there is a problem, or even if it is doing an exceptionally good job blocking malware. Why would you essentially pick a consumer-grade antivirus solution for your enterprise-grade environment? Unfortunately, this happens all the time, and we end up with the "bolt-on" approach to solve the problem. And even when it does alert, it fails to collect the required information to properly mitigate the threat based on data from all three pillars.

As we stabilize our cybersecurity best practices and focus on basic security hygiene, consider the longer-term goals of your business. If you choose a vendor that does not operate across these three pillars and has no integration strategy to promote interoperation and data exchange, it is truly a point solution, and you should be fully aware of the risks.

Everything we choose as a security solution should benefit the integration of these pillars; if they do not, then ask a lot of questions. For example, why would you choose a particular camera system without centralized management capabilities? It falls into the asset protection pillar and can monitor physical access by an identity, but without centralized capabilities and management, it is a standalone silo not supporting your foundation. It needs to support all three pillars to be an effective security solution and, ultimately, provide useful information for correlation, analytics, and adaptive response.

Some may argue that there could be four or even five pillars for a sound cybersecurity defense. They could be education, partners, and so on to support your foundation. We prefer to think of all tools and solutions in these three categories. Why?

A three-legged stool never wobbles! And, each of these has documented attack vectors that can be managed as integrated pillars. Those are the basis for our other books, *Privileged Attack Vectors* and *Asset Attack Vectors*.

While it's no secret that identifying and correcting network security holes is critical to protecting any business from harmful attacks, the processes of privileged access management, vulnerability assessment, and configuration management often get overlooked as a critical component for sound security practices affecting assets. This is basic cybersecurity hygiene. To that end, vulnerability management should be an ongoing process, but too often organizations are lazy in maintaining a proper vulnerability workflow and only react when disaster strikes and they are forced to inspect the process in detail. Even then, some businesses fail to learn the lesson of proactive vulnerability assessment and remediation and are behind in managing all three pillars. You cannot protect an identity well when the asset itself can be exploited.

Additionally, many organizations look at vulnerability management in isolation. Take a step back and look at the wealth of asset and risk information that is captured in a vulnerability scan. Usually this includes everything from vulnerabilities to accounts and groups available to the local asset. Examine how this data can not only help prioritize patches and mobilize IT resources but also be applied to strengthen other security investments across the organization, including asset management, patch management, application control, analytics, and threat detection – to name a few, based on the raw diversity of the data itself. This information can even help you strengthen your identity posture by locating the presence of appropriate and inappropriate (rogue) accounts across your organization. It is yet another tool that helps you with the challenges and strategies outlined further in this book and managing identity attack vectors.

CHAPTER 2

A Nuance on Lateral Movement

To a threat actor, lateral movement means all the difference between compromising a single resource and potentially navigating throughout an organization to establish a persistent presence. Their goal is to remain undetected and ultimately conduct their nefarious mission even if some defenses manage to track their infiltration. While the hacker might succeed based on an opportunistic phishing attack or a targeted attack based on stolen credentials or an exploit, lateral movement is the means to find data of value, compromise additional assets, execute malware, and ultimately own accounts and identities to continue their attack. Lateral movement, by the most traditional definition, is the ability to pivot from one resource to another and to navigate among other resources in any environment. The key takeway for our conversation today, and why we need to talk about lateral movement, is not about assets however; it is about "resources" since they can be so much more than just computers and applications.

Resources engaged in lateral movement can be any one of the following and, most importantly, any combination of them too. This is documented in Table 2-1 along with the most common privileged and asset attack vectors.

© Morey J. Haber, Darran Rolls 2020
M. J. Haber and D. Rolls, *Identity Attack Vectors*, https://doi.org/10.1007/978-1-4842-5165-2_2

Table 2-1. *Resource lateral movement techniques*

Resources	Privileged Attack Vector	Asset Attack Vector
Operating system	Credential, certifcates, or hash-based attacks	Vulnerabilities, exploits, and misconfigurations
Applications	Credential, certifcates, or application-to-application attacks	Vulnerabilities, exploits, misconfigurations, insecure architectures, and end of life
Containers	Credential, certifcates, or insecure connectivity (lack of zero trust)	Vulnerabilities, exploits, misconfigurations, insecure architectures, and agile DevOps
Virtual machines	Credential or hash- or hypervisor-based credential attacks	Vulnerabilities, exploits, misconfigurations, insecure architectures and agile DevOps, and CPU- and memory-based vulnerabilities
Accounts	Credential theft or abuse or identity theft	Credential theft, abuse, memory-scraping, and insecure credential storage
Identities	Credential reuse, credential theft	Inappropriate account linkage

While the techniques for lateral movement vary greatly between these resources including privileged and asset attack vectors, the objective is the same – to laterally move between resources that are similar or share underlying services. That is, you can laterally move from an operating system to an application and then compromise additional accounts using any combination of the attack vectors (and there are definitely more) referenced in the preceding text. This raises the obvious question, how to protect against lateral movement when it can occur in so many different ways and between so many different things?

First, consider the underlying faults that allow lateral movement to occur. They occur due to privileged attacks or asset attacks and ultimately can own an identity. The latter is typically accomplished through vulnerability, patch, and configuration management. These are traditional cybersecurity best practices that every organization should be doing well, but in reality, as we all know, very few have them working like well-oiled machines. The conversation we need to have with our teams is that lateral movement, due to poor basic cybersecurity hygiene, is the primary attack vector for modern threats like ransomware, bots, worms, and other malware. Contemporary concepts like zero trust and just-in-time identity and privileged access management cannot mitigate the threats from asset attack vectors. A successful attack is based on software flaws and not credentials used for the interaction of resources. Therefore, for lateral movement based on asset attacks, we need to ensure the basics are being done well week after week, month after month, and year over year to ensure we do not expose cracks in our security posture that could lead to a vulnerability and exploit combination.

The second method of lateral movement is based on privileged attack vectors. This typically includes some form of privileged remote access and, in today's world, is the easiest attack vector for a threat actor to own a resource and conduct lateral movement. These techniques include:

- Password guessing

- Dictionary attacks

- Brute force attacks (including techniques like password spraying)

- Pass the hash

- Security questions

- Password reset

- Multifactor authentication flaws

- Default credentials

- Backdoor credentials

- Anonymous access

- Predictable password creation

- Shared credentials

- Temporary password

- Reused or recycled passwords

This is where the concepts of zero trust and just-in-time privileged access management actually do help in mitigating threats.

- Zero trust is a security model based on the principle of maintaining strict access controls and not trusting anyone, anywhere, at any time, even those already inside the network perimeter, by default.

- Just-in-time privileged access is a strategy that aligns real-time requests for usage of privileged accounts directly with entitlements, workflow, and appropriate access policies.

The mitigation from either of these is relatively straightforward. Ensure that authorization or authentication is not allowed between resources unless a third-party trust and approval has been granted and access control between resources is modified using ephemeral properties guaranteeing that any potential trust that allows lateral movement is not persistent. Remember lateral movement can happen in between resources and it is that inappropriate trust between them that should be prevented in order to mitigate the threats of lateral movement. This almost always occurs between resources, at any layer, when poor credential, identity, and password management disciplines are attack vectors. This is why Identity Governance is so important to manage this risk.

To that end, lateral movement is much more than moving from asset to asset inappropriately by a threat actor. In reality, it is lateral movement between any resource using either privileged or asset attack vectors. And, if multiple accounts are compromised for the same identity, then the attack vector can truly evolve into an identity attack vector in which everything a person owns, is responsible for, or has privileged or unprivileged access to becomes a form of lateral movement based on the account/identity relationship. This is important in our conversation about lateral movement because the resource is not always electronic. It can be abstract like an identity, bot, or software in the form of a container or DevOps. Regardless, the movement from a threat actor is a pivot and critical to their malicious intent.

CHAPTER 3

The Five A's of Enterprise IAM

There are lots of frameworks to help you define, organize, implement, and improve security. Initiatives like the Control Objectives for Information and Related Technology (COBIT), the US National Institute of Standards and Technology (NIST) Cybersecurity Framework, and the International Organization for Standardization (ISO) 27K all provide frameworks to guide security program thinking. They are frameworks, because they provide extensive guidance on everything from funding to security incident response readiness.

One of the greatest challenges all security frameworks face is their complexity. Identity Management is part of most, if not all, "official" security frameworks. Identity is often a section, sometimes a chapter, but never the focus. In an effort to simplify things for this publication, rather than choosing a single framework and pulling out identity, we instead offer our own focused mini-framework called the "The Five A's of Enterprise IAM." Figure 3-1 shows an overview of this concept. It offers a stripped-down definition and scope for how we now see Identity Management as a set of universal principles that apply to all of the established security frameworks and to just about all enterprise security scenarios. The Five A's cover Authentication, Authorization, Administration, Audit, and Analytics – each is explained in detail in the following. Once you gain a mastery of the Five A's, you will be ready to deliver identity management operational controls in just about any scenario for virtually any type of organization or vertical industry focus.

© Morey J. Haber, Darran Rolls 2020
M. J. Haber and D. Rolls, *Identity Attack Vectors*, https://doi.org/10.1007/978-1-4842-5165-2_3

Figure 3-1. *The Five A's of Identity Management*

Authentication

Authentication is often confused with authorization even though they are distinct technologies and practices. In some computing models, authentication and authorization are blended together and have little distinction or separation in implementation or management. Apple iOS, for example, uses biometrics for both authorization and authentication, and the end-user experience is blurred regardless of the action type. By definition, authentication is a login (username) in addition to some form of secret, historically a password, to establish proof or trust in an identity. It is essentially a validation of who you say you are.

Authentication of your identity = login + shared secret (password)

While there are countless variations of shared secrets that can be used within a login, such as pin codes, passwords, keys, two-factor authentication, and so on, the login itself is generally not a secret and often guessable for an identity. For example, login could be "jtitor" for my alias as an abbreviation of John Titor's name. However, a login could also be something more complex like an employee number, which better masks a user's identity. For highly secure environments, this second approach is preferable, especially for administrator or root accounts. You do not visually identify the privileges with the account simply by looking at the account or username. Obscurity is not security but it often helps!

So, in simple terms, authentication is nothing more than proving your identity or you ownership of a given account. It does not provide permissions, privileges, or access, just confirmation that you are who you say you are.

Authorization

Authorization is the next step after authentication. You cannot be authorized to perform a function, have privileges assigned, or even perform tasks in a given role, without some form of authentication happening first. Even if you are a Guest in an application or operating system and have no login and/or password of your own, your authentication is assumed to be Guest, and you are granted all the rights and privileges of that Guest. The login username and password secret are therefore much less relevant, but you have still been authenticated and have still been assigned some form of authorization, albeit very little.

> *Authorization = privileges (what you are allowed to do) + authentication*

Authorization is, therefore, the right to perform a function based on your authentication. Your identity and its associated account are granted privileges to perform specific functions and may also be explicitly denied or not privileged to perform other functions. These privileges can be assigned within an application, an operating system, or some part of the supporting infrastructure. It could also be assigned within an identity or privilege management system that is controlling it. In order to manage at scale, the latter is always recommended.

When like privileges are grouped together, they create the foundation of a Role. When a Role is assigned to a group of accounts, the Role is providing authorization for that group to perform those functions.

In the case of a mobile device like an Apple iPhone running iOS, facial recognition or fingerprint touch is used for both authentication and authorization. They will log you into the device (authentication), and they can also be used to secure payments or to make purchases – very specifically an authorization – it does so using the same mechanisms.

In today's world of high-fidelity cybersecurity, using the same mechanism or technique for both authentication and authorization at the same time can lead to significant issues relating to the integrity, controls, and oversight for the process, and many in the industry now believe they should be kept separate. A breach or weakness in one model leads to a breach or weakness in the other. While Apple has designed high levels of security into their solutions to minimize the risk, in general, most computing environments should avoid using the same technology for authentication and authorization. Just because you have been authenticated does not mean you should have authorization. Those privileges and permissions should ultimately be decided upon using a separate process and a separate layer in the security stack. Even in modern "state-of-the-art" computing environments, we often see the same lack of separation when a Single Sign-On (SSO) solution blurs the line between initial authentication and the automatic authorization within a managed application. Multifactor authentication (MFA) solutions can help mitigate this risk by requiring a second validation for privileged authorization activity.

Administration

Search the Internet, and you'll find 100 different definitions for administration. In the context of this book, we are very specifically talking about the administration of authentication, authorization, and audit controls. Administration here means configuration management and governance controls over any changes made to that authentication, authorization, and audit. In Chapter 6 on Identity Governance Defined, we explain how providing a centralized and normalized set of administration capabilities for all access systems can help; this is the mandate of Identity Governance.

Authentication and Authorization mechanisms are inherently distributed, painfully diverse, and perpetually changing. After 25 years of watching this space develop, most "old-timers" in the IAM space are usually quite retrospect about how much things have changed, but yet how much they are still the same. Most organizations still struggle to get full administrative control over the systems and data they are responsible for protecting. It is therefore essential, in our view, that Administration is treated independently from the ever-changing mix of AuthN (**auth**entication) and AuthZ (**auth**orization) technologies. You might say "stick to your knitting" is the name of the administration game. Don't just let Authentication or Authorization manage it. That way, through specialization and focus, you might actually get true administrative coverage.

IAM administration is a big part of the Identity Governance remit. Add to it Audit and Analytics (in the following), and you have the product scope of most enterprise-class Identity Governance solutions. Through the use of a dedicated heterogeneous management approach, Identity Governance strives to take on the mantle of global administration, audit, and analytics for all users and all data access. By leveraging the Identity Governance processes (also outlined in Chapter 7), administration can provide visibility, controls, automation, and full lifecycle management (LCM) of all users and their access.

Audit

Facilitating the delivery of a repeatable and sustainable user access, Audit process is also the responsibility of the Identity Governance process. Whether it is overlaying specific controls to meet regulatory compliance, or creating system-driven lifecycle management functions that are stable and verifiable as controls proof, Audit is a significant part of the identity management system.

For some, the Audit of IAM means delivering a user access certification program. For others, it's defining and implementing preventive and detective policy such as Separation of Duty (SoD). For all, it is being able to prove that comprehensive administration processes and policies are in place and being adhered to.

Analytics

The fifth and final A is the comprehensive analysis of how the IAM system is operating. Analytics means gaining operational and security insights, through the ongoing collection and processing of identity-related configuration, assignment, and usage data.

Advanced identity analytics enables a more informed and predictive approach to governance. Using Machine Learning (ML) and Artificial Intelligence (AI) techniques, identity analytics tools can provide important peer-group analysis information that helps to extend identity audit and administration functions and make them more dynamic and responsive. For example, if an analytics engine discovers suspicious, inappropriate, or unusual access, it can prompt administrators to review that access to ensure that the correct configuration has been implemented. Analytics can provide auto-generated insights and recommendations that allow the line of business to make more informed access decisions that enhance operational security and ensure compliance. With the advancements in ML and AI, mass quantities of operational data can now be discovered and processed to uncover hidden insights and actionable guidance far beyond what a traditional rules-based engine can achieve.

CHAPTER 4

Understanding Enterprise Identity

The French philosopher Rene Descartes is credited for stating "Cogito, ergo sum." In English, it translates into "I think, therefore, I am." This statement is profoundly responsible for thousands of hours of Philosophy 101 classes and for discussions on the meaning of life and the existence of a human soul. One thing is certain from this quote: "I think, therefore, I am" can also mean you have an Identity.

Barring any philosophical discussions on the meaning of life (and a quick shout-out to Monty Python) and the existence of a human soul, an Identity is typically a one-to-one relationship between a human being (a carbon-based life form) and their digital presence. Their digital presence, however, can have multiple accounts, multiple credentials, and an infinite number of entitlements in its electronic format. For example, consider the accounts associated with your enterprise identity. These account names might be comprised of your first initial and last name, or obfuscated by using some form of patterned letters and numbers. It could also be a random alias like "JTitor" which, unless you have a mapping back to your real identity, has no logical meaning to anyone outside of yourself. It is considered an Identity Access Management best practice to permanently map this identifier back to your identity.

In some environments, however, an Identity may deviate from this best practice and not require a human mapping presence. An Identity can represent a defined resource, an asset, or even an automated robot process. This extended definition allows for the fact that complete computerized systems can take on a life of their own and, thus, can be assigned an Identity even though they do not "think."

While this extended definition is not common (yet) and shares a different definition for cloud-based identity models like those seen in the Amazon Web Services (AWS) environment, it does represent an interesting direction in this technology and the personification of traits we place upon our creations. This advanced form of an identity

© Morey J. Haber, Darran Rolls 2020
M. J. Haber and D. Rolls, *Identity Attack Vectors*, https://doi.org/10.1007/978-1-4842-5165-2_4

should not be confused with accounts or credentials used for service accounts or a shared administrator access in some subsystem. To better explain this, think of it like a robot or humanoid. If your office has invested in mail robots, or extensively deployed office automation technology, these processes may (or may not) look human or may be even look like a creepier version of R2D2 from *Star Wars*. These assets have an automated mission and have some form of unique identification. Therefore, R2D2 or C3PO are valid identities, even though they are not flesh and blood. The accounts and credentials they use to operate their functions should be linked back to their identities. After all, how did R2D2 authenticate to the Death Star computer to find Princess Leia without a valid credential? Leia's location absolutely was privileged information, so maybe R2D2 had access to a stolen account to perform his query. In this sense, both are a part of an identity attack vector.

Today, real-world discussions of Identities are translatable to you and me, and the future cannot ignore that Identities assigned to a machine (or resource) are also a potential attack vector. For the purposes of this book, Identities can mean either a person – but with always a one-to-one relationship – or a technology implementation, with the potential to be a one-to-many relationship. "I think, therefore, I am" is one identity, and a machine (mail robot), even if there are dozens within a building, should have only one identity. Unfortunately, in practical implementations, organizations may find this not true. Individual machine identities as security best practice should never be shared, even though their accounts and credentials may be shared. Shared credentials are a security taboo, but may be needed for a technology implementation to succeed due limitations in the technology itself. Thus, machine implementations of identities may have an undesirable one-to-many relationship too.

This leads us to the evolution of identities as an attack vector beyond assets, people, and machines and the privileges being leveraged as attack vectors within an identity.

People and Persona

When working with indicators of compromise (IoCs), we always want to try to map a given anomaly back to a specific account, credential, and identity. This enables us to focus on the root cause and build effective defenses and policies.

A persona is a derivative of an Identity and refers to a special situation in which a person has multiple identities each of a different "class." A good example comes from the healthcare provider space. Here it's quite common to see a clinician (with the accounts and privileges associated with being a doctor), who is also a patient at the same facility. Each persona has multiple accounts, but the doctor and the patient personas are not linked together in any part of the account or sign-on infrastructure. In fact, quite the opposite, they are intentionally separated from each other.

For an identity as an attack vector, threat actors will target a persona and exploit weaknesses in how these account relationships are managed. This could be targeting teams responsible for a specific function like accounting or accounts payable, with a specific malicious phishing email such as a fraudulent wire transfer. It could be targeting Human Resources (HR) with a malicious file or fake resume targeting a vulnerability to exploit a system. So a persona refers to a logical grouping of people at a high level independent of their privileges and resources and at slightly lower grouping than their roles (discussed later).

A persona can be looked at as the groupings of identities targeted for an attack at the highest generic level of their job description. That can be anything from sales to executives and include any potential group your organization may have. Identity attacks will typically focus on a specific group in a targeted campaign, such as with broad spear-phishing campaigns to individuals in that group. This is why personas are so important in relation to identities. They are used for everything from legitimate sales cycles to help vendors and marketing find the right buyers through targeted attacks leveraging the responsibilities of the persona to perpetrate an assault.

Therefore, personas are directly translated into Roles within an IAM solution in order to electronically document a group of identities' responsibilities. While they are technically not the same, this perspective is helpful while maturing your Identity Governance model.

Physical Persona

A physical persona refers to when a logical persona is reflected into the physical world. In the real world, there are sometimes physical traits that are connected to your persona. For example, these could be the uniforms we wear and the types and colors of badges we use for authorization. Physical identity threats are commonly depicted in movies when actors wear specific uniforms to breach an environment and impersonate a persona in order to gain access. If you ever have had a physical penetration test performed on your environment, this is one potential attack vector. A janitor's uniform, or even wearing a suit, might be sufficient to circumvent physical defenses and breach an environment. It is just another identity-based attack vector since physical appearance is sometimes enough to fool an unsuspecting victim.

Electronic Persona

An electronic persona is the digital translation of your physical persona. It is conceptually a subset of a Role (explained in Chapter 7) and differs only in hierarchy. An electronic persona is the many-to-one translation of identities into a digital form, while a Role is the high-level grouping of the persona at a functional level.

For example, John is an employee. John works in a hospital and has the appropriate clothing for his job as a lab technician (physical persona). His position is a medical lab technician for processing bloodwork, but his electronic persona may be restricted to a grouping of technicians for a certain floor, types of tests, or even data that the technician may be able to access. His persona explains his job, but the Role is the association of applicable functions he is entitled too along with his peers. In many cases, his electronic persona may have entitlements unique to only him, and not assigned to anyone else. Common entitlements should be associated by Role. Therefore, his electronic persona is a lab technician (job title), and his Role provides common work functions among his peers.

This creates an interesting risk as an identity attack vector. The threats against an electronic persona with unique entitlements are different from a group of individuals with similar rights. If only one person is the database administrator, their electronic persona is the only one susceptible to a privileged attack vector. The database and server are susceptible to an asset attack vector (vulnerabilities and exploits). If a larger group of people is granted database administrative rights, they all would be susceptible to an attack. Performing an analysis of entitlements (certification) is much easier on groups of people versus individuals. However, assigning broad rights to everyone violates the principle of least privilege and introduces excessive risk.

Organizations may choose to use job titles or business roles to establish this foundation, but keep in mind that the entitlements assigned relative to a business role and a persona are not equal. That is, not everyone with the title "engineer" should be treated the same even though that is their electronic persona. For example, all engineers may have the same laptop image and installed tools, but not the same accounts and entitlements based on their department and responsibilities.

To better understand the difference between electronic and physical personas, Table 4-1 compares them from a criminal perspective. It explains how physical crimes translate to electronic crimes and why mitigation steps are needed to prevent them.

Table 4-1. *Physical to electronic crime comparison*

Physical Persona Crimes	Electronic Persona Crimes
Burglary – Physical breaking and entering and the theft of material goods	*Hacking* – Electronic intrusion using unauthorized access to steal or alter information
Deceptive, vPhishing (Voice or VoIP Phishing), or prank callers – Audible crimes using telephones targeting end users directly or organizations like banks	*Phishing or SMSishing* – Electronic crimes using emails or SMS text messages to socially engineer the end user to expose credentials, passwords, or other sensitive information
Extortion – Illegal use of force and position to obtain funds, property, or other material objects of value	*Data extortion* – The hacking of sensitive information and threating the release of data unless funds are paid. This is typically in the form of bitcoins and includes ransomware
Fraud – Dishonest activities used to perform deception of targeted organizations or people for financial or other monetary gains	*Web-based fraud* – A broad category that encompasses web sites and other Internet communications to defraud an individual of sensitive information or credentials to gain access. This category is typically linked with phishing and other online chat types of attacks
Identity theft – The physical impersonation of another individual to gain access or defraud an individual or organization	*Identity theft* – The electronic theft of an identity using accounts to impersonate a user and steal information or defraud them of money
Child exploitation – Criminal victimization of minors for indecent motives	*Child exploitation* – The electronic distribution of images and information relating to victims who are minors

This is where Identity Access Management (IAM) solutions can help implement safeguards in a digital world. An enterprise-class IAM solution will help by managing the relationships between identities, accounts, and privileges and by helping model and manage logical persona and the classification of people.

Accounts

An account is an electronic representation of an identity and can have a one-to-many relationship with the identity. One identity can, therefore, have multiple accounts. These accounts reference a set of permissions and privileges needed for an application or asset to connect or operate within the confines of a resource. While the definition of an account is obvious for an identity, it can take on a variety of forms when used electronically for services, impersonations, and application-to-application functions.

Accounts can have complex relationships with identities and can be defined locally, grouped together, nested in groups, or managed via identity infrastructure such as directory services. Accounts can have role-based access applied to them either directly, at the group level, or based on a directory entry. These roles can implement a wide range of capabilities–from disabling access, to providing privileged capabilities such as root, local administrator, or domain admin. The level of privileges and role-based access is dependent on the security model of the system implementing them and can vary significantly from one implementation to another.

Linking accounts to identities is how we gain access to information technology resources. Technically, any account is simply a vehicle to authorize usage and control operational parameters. Excessive assignment of privileges to any given account goes against the principle of least privilege and will greatly increase cyber risk and the potential for a privileged attack vector.

Credentials

A credential is an account with an associated password, passcode, certificate, or other types of key. Credentials can have more than one security mechanism assigned to them – this is called dual or multifactor authentication. Credentials can also be shared and used anonymously. In the case of an anonymous account, the credentials use a null password. This is different than a guest account.

Credentials are simply the representation of the account and authentication secret combination used for authentication. They are, nonetheless, the crown jewels for any threat actor to begin an escalation of privileges.

When someone has "hacked" an account, what it really means is that they have taken over control of the credentials associated with the account. Literally hacking an account would only yield a username. Both the username and password are needed to successfully compromise a credential and potentially anything that credential protects.

For simplicity's sake, in the remainder of this book, hacking an account means the same thing as taking control of its credentials. It is difficult enough managing privileges in an environment without having to parse the semantics used every day in describing the threat. However, security professionals and the press will probably never change in saying one million accounts were compromised when, in fact, one million credentials where compromised. See the difference? The account was compromised because the credentials were exposed in some form of breach or attack.

Realizations

Today in the technology world, we repeatedly hear buzzwords such as "digital transformation," "zero trust," "Identity Governance," and "just-in-time access." The implementation of our digital identities in the business world has become an essential prerequisite for doing even the basic tasks in most enterprises. Everything from walking into an office building and scanning a badge to punching a time clock at a construction site requires identities, access, and privileges.

Our electronic identities are everywhere, while our physical personas remain rooted with who we are and what we do; our logical personas are far more transient. The combination of the physical and the logical is what identity attack vectors play upon. At the heart of every identity are privileges. If you can compromise an identity, then you assume its privileges. If you can elevate your privileges to root or administrator, you can own an asset. If you own the asset, you can manipulate the data and software to conduct nefarious activities. Therefore, we are back to our three pillars of security, and our implementations must start with strong protections and separations for an identity.

The simplest real-world example of this in the United States is the one-to-one relationship between an identity and a Social Security number (SSN). Social Security numbers are considered personally identifiable information (PII) and, if linked to a person's name, can be used in identity theft. Opening a credit card and potentially tampering with someone's mortgage or property title are all possible if a threat actor knows the victim's SSN and a few other tidbits of information like their address and date of birth. Therefore, keeping an SSN safe, secure, and secret is critical to protecting one's identity.

Not all countries follow the same model of secrecy with their national identifiers. In some countries, the SSN equivalent is not private, but rather public so that any person can be documented, tracked, or identified by their unique designation. In these countries, possessing a person's national identity number and their name is not sufficient to initiate an identity theft attack. Sadly, due to weakness in the current banking, government, and Social Security system in the United States, this information, blended with basic information like a victim's email address, is more than enough to begin an attack.

This leads us to an interesting conclusion. A secure implementation of an identity-based system should not have a single point of failure, like a social security number. Any identity-based system should be resilient to this type of attack – a high-level concept we will continue to explore and provide guidance on how to implement within your organization throughout this book.

Users

As we have defined, Identities are typically associated one-to-one with users (people). Users can have multiple accounts, credentials, and even personas, but they have only one identity.

If a threat actor can insert himself into that one-to-one relationship, then we likely have an incident. Therefore, the most effective strategy is to protect the relationship and eliminate single points of failure for a user (not a persona), like our SSN example. The representation for an identity should be a designator with little or no value and should not be directly linked to any other form of identification. For a successful implementation of this relationship, consider the following:

- Identity designators for a person should never be used for authorization or authentication.

- Identity designators are only for reference and can be alphanumeric, symbolic, electronic, or biometric in representation (the risks of biometric are covered in Chapter 19).

- Storage of the designators should be protected even if they are public. They are still PII since they can be linked backed to a person.

- These are commonly implemented in businesses using the concept of employee identification numbers.

Although a single account reference may be an annoyance if compromised, a database of central designators can reveal way more about the overall security system and should always be safeguarded. Most modern breaches reveal this information in the simplest form, like an email address.

In most organizations today, the most common implementation of an identity (user) source, outside of an HR record, is in a directory service of accounts in the form of a security identifier (SID). In the context of a Microsoft Windows operating system, a SID is a unique, immutable identifier for an account reference, user group, and credential. It is not the same as a company's employee number, but does have a relationship back through an account to the same identity.

An account should have a single, immutable SID for the life of the account (at least in a given Active Directory domain), and all properties of the identity, including its name, account, attributes, and so on, are associated with the SID. This is even true for just-in-time access, but the SID is only "alive" for the authorized task or mission. This design allows a principal/account to be renamed (e.g., from "John Titor" to "Morey Haber") without affecting the account and the security attributes of objects that refer to the identity. The SID alone is not enough to compromise the integrity of the relationship without some other external factors. This helps meet the requirements outlined in the preceding text, but unfortunately, a SID can be used for authentication when paired with a valid password or hash.

It is important to note that not all technology implementations use the concept of an identity to implement their functions or services. For example, an IoT camera likely has just one account that operates as an administrator of the device. The relationship between the user and the camera skips the concept of an identity and persona and maps straight from the user to the camera's administration account. Not everyone should be a camera administrator. In addition, other employees may know those credentials, making it a one-to-many relationship for any technology implementation. The camera has no concept of an identity unless it has technology implemented for role-based access (RBAC) that allows it to link back to multiple accounts and granularity of privileges.

This takes the concept of the identity to the highest level, a person (people). The mappings to an employee number, accounts, and SID are all a part of their identity as an electronic persona.

Applications

To be fair, the concept of applications having unique identities is controversial in the information technology community. A payroll system, web application, or even an engineering database should not have an identity. The application will have various accounts that, in turn, will have owners in order to operate the application correctly – but the application itself will likely not have an identity.

However, this is where a new gray area begins. What about a bot? It is a software-based application that impersonates a person and has a persona. It may be backed by artificial intelligence (AI) to provide automated responses and may actually be linked to a true person's identity as its owner. Should it have an identity of its own? There is no simple, universally agreed upon answer to this question, but in our opinion, it should have one as it is mimicking human traits and should be classified as another electronic persona. Figure 4-1 illustrates a bot commonly found on the Internet interacting with people to explain this type of outlier. Is it a person or an application responding to you?

Figure 4-1. *Automated chat bot*

If we consider that this type of application has an identity, its implementation should be governed by the following principles:

- Application identities should be assigned when the software emulates human behavior or can interoperate with a person on its own accord.

- All application identities should have human owner(s) assigned to them since they are not truly sentient beings, but need to be managed through a controls lifecycle.

- Application identities should follow all the same criteria as human identities except:

  - Their personas should be strictly limited to only the tasks they can perform. For example, there is no reason for a bot to have access to the same systems a human being does, such as local login rights, or access to the parking garage. Their privileges must be assigned separately and in accordance with established Identity Governance lifecycle policies.

  - Application logs should be strictly monitored for any privileged access occurring outside of their designated tasks. This activity would represent an indicator of compromise and, as an example, was cited in the first half of 2018 in a credit card breach for a major airline.

  - The relationship of an application to its identity should be one to one at the lowest level possible. For example, each fictitious bot used in a chat conversation may not have a unique identity, even though the name and picture are random to the end user. It appears to be separate people. The instantiation of the bots owns the identity in lieu of each chat instance. If it is possible, each chat instance should have an identity since it operates and emulates a person independently. However, this may not be technically feasible based on your implementation. For instance, it may not scale to the number of applications executing dynamically. Just consider the assignment of an identity at the lowest level possible. This will help digital forensics investigations, should they ever be needed.

For your environment, assigning identities to applications is truly a business and technical decision. As a best practice recommendation, consider why you would need to have an identity and when is it appropriate. A good rule of thumb is, if it emulates a human or starts to emulate Skynet (shout-out to the *Terminator*), it needs an identity of its own. And, try to keep the relationship one to one. Any forensics or usage analysis looking for indicators of compromise will depend on that uniqueness. And for the sake of an identity, make sure one of its attributes is an owner that can map it back to a human identity. We will cover this in more detail in the next sections.

Machines

In a modern office, you may see robots delivering mail or even an IoT device brewing coffee. Machines have a combination of hardware and software that may require an identity to govern their operations, ownership, and autonomy. Deciding whether an identity should be assigned to a machine is more complicated than just a decision of an identity for an application. Our chat bot example illustrates this and makes machine-based identity decisions even trickier based on their real-world interactions.

Consider a smart coffee maker. The word "smart" implies it is network-enabled and an IoT asset. Should it have an identity? Well, that all depends on the coffee maker. An IoT model can brew coffee, notify you if coffee grounds need to be added or if waste needs to be removed, or if there is another issue. It may act more like a robot and, therefore, should have an identity. Conversely, if the coffee maker just sets a timer and sends alerts, even though it is an IoT machine, does it really need an identity? Probably not but if it can be attacked, and its operating system can be owned via an asset attack vector, or its administrator account compromised via a privileged attack vector, it is a risk. Personifying an identity for it becomes a business choice. There is no rule that it should or shouldn't have one, even if it authenticates on the network to perform its tasks.

Let's consider a more detailed example. Let's explore our physical mail robot again. It travels floor-to-floor to deliver old-school, paper-based mail and packages. For all purposes, it is an autonomous robot, has ownership assigned to a team, and has an identity. This mail robot is behaving like a persona with a very specific set of tasks: get and deliver mail. This is much like a summer job for many of us "old-timers."

In our scenario, the mail robot is an asset of the company, can have physical and software vulnerabilities, and has defined privileges required in order to perform its job. These privileges could include access to the mail room and to specialized elevators to travel between floors. However, for one reason or another, it does not have privileges to the same elevators and hallways used by the human workforce. Sound feasible right? We have established this asset does have an identity based on these traits. What could its identity attack vectors be?

- Misrouting of mail to threat actors
- Physical harm based on inappropriate movement

- Inappropriate access by a threat actor to cameras and logs for surveillance

- Transport of illegal, inappropriate, or stolen material in and out, or through, an office

These could be potentially devastating attacks. This is why the mail robot needs an identity. It can be tricked into behaving like a threat actor (insider or external threat) and leveraged against the business in ways we have not let conceived of. It can be compromised in ways that impact the physical or electronic integrity of your environment and possibly impact a human with the same persona.

This scenario leads us to an interesting conclusion. Machines should be assigned identities when their risks can mimic a human persona – electronic or physical. These can be quantified in a risk analysis assessment beyond just a compromise or data breach. Identities should not be assigned to machines when the risks are strictly electronic, and attack vectors are similar to any other network device. The decision between assigning an identity or not is a gray area, but an IoT coffee maker is just that – a coffee maker. There is no reason to complicate the situation with over-assignment, but if something mimics human behavior, it should have an identity. R2D2 surely does, and as you will read, he has an owner too, and he did have real-world physical interactions.

Ownership

Every identity requires an owner. If you are a human being, you are your own owner. It sounds silly, but when an identity is assigned to an application or machine, it gets an additional attribute of an owner or owners. This is conceptually the same as having a supervisor or manager assigned for human identities; however, for non-carbon-based life forms, there are a few additional traits to consider:

- The owners of a machine or application identity are responsible for its runtime. Owners are not necessarily in charge of the resource's lifecycle, maintenance, and behavior. This is the same as being a parent or guardian of a potentially mischievous minor.

- Ownership can be a one-to-many relationship and not explicitly assigned to a single person. Ownership can be assigned to teams, departments, or even other entities outside of the organization.

- Owners have explicit control over their identities and their associated technology implementation. This includes everything from cradle-to-grave operations of the identity and its usage.

- Owners are basically responsible. In the world of corporate responsibility and audit, being able to assign ownership and responsibility is key to defining and maintaining controls and oversight.

Automation

Identities can operate autonomously or be under strict control and supervision. This includes everything from their automated creation through to their eventual revocation. Automation becomes key when identities are being managed using Identity Access Management (IAM) or Identity Governance and Administration (IGA) solutions.

Automation relies on establishing known responsibilities. Understanding what some automation should do is a prerequisite to giving it the power to go do it for itself. Many of the challenges associated with automation for identity management can be solved when the concept of personas is expanded to include the concept of Roles. Roles are a means of grouping people and privileges to form groupings that simplify the assignment of entitlement based on common technical or business functions. An identity can be placed into a Role (this concept will be covered later) to automate the entitlement assignment based on this grouping. Using Roles, a human identity can be assigned accounts, users, entitlements, privileges, and asset assignments using automation software. If a machine or application entitlement is required, then the appropriate entitlements AND ownership assignment can be automated as well. Once the identity is established, the automation of all its entitlement can be controlled in a predictable and sustainable fashion.

If you had to make these assignments manually and decide which people and which machines should have an identity based on their inception, there would be inconsistencies in your implementation. Automation simplifies classification in a consistent way and helps enforce best practices across the physical and logic environment.

Types of Accounts

Identities can be assigned a wide variety of accounts across the enterprise. Accounts can be of many different types and use a wide variety of techniques (well outside the scope of this book) to enforce credentials, control entitlement, and govern access.

If a single account is compromised, it can be used to compromise the entire identity and all of its privileges. For instance, the compromise of an account with administrator access, or some other high-level application privilege, can easily be leveraged against the identity to compromise other associated accounts and services. This is often referred to as account-based lateral movement when a threat actor leverages one privileged account against another linked by a single identity.

To reduce the likelihood and impact of attacks that abuse or escalate privileges, we should always strive to restrict the assignment of privileges to the lowest common denominator for every type of account. This concept is called least privilege and should, whenever possible, be implemented on all account types to help avoid an account-level attack from escalating back to the identity itself. Figure 4-2 illustrates the often complex account and identity relationships that exist in most enterprise environments.

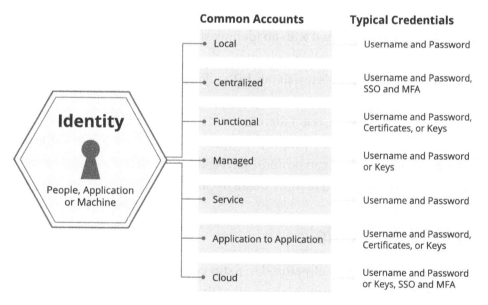

Figure 4-2. Basic identity, account, and credential relationship

In the next section, we will cover the most prevalent account types, how they are typically implemented, and how they can be used to compromise an identity.

Local Accounts

Local accounts are just that, local to the resource or asset. They may, or may not, be centrally managed or referenced in an identity management solution. Duplicate accounts with the same credentials often exist across similar assets and should be discovered, cataloged, and managed in order to govern their access. If duplicate local accounts do exist and they are using the same passwords, the system is likely exposed to significant privileged attack vectors and lateral movement. Therefore, local accounts should where possible have unique usernames and always have different credentials. If the usernames can be changed and made unique, this can create a management problem due to the sheer number of accounts that needed to be managed. This challenge can easily be addressed by using the kinds of IGA and Privileged Access Management (PAM) solutions discussed in this book.

If the duplicate local accounts do have high-level privileged access, a compromise of the credentials could lead to the complete compromise of the asset. If other resources share those accounts and credentials, privileged lateral movement will most likely occur and, consequently, escalation from the account to the identity as we explained before. Once the identity is owned, all accounts associated with the identity can potentially be compromised as well. Local account creation should, therefore, support least privilege, and each instantiation associated with an identity should have unique credentials to prevent these types of attacks.

To illustrate this further, let's revisit our IoT coffee maker, which has a local administrative account built into its management software called "admin." Changing the username may not be possible, but if there is more than one coffee maker within your organization, each should have a unique password. Managing those passwords is a very well-understood problem and can be addressed using a Privileged Access Management (PAM) solution. PAM is covered in more detail in Chapter 13.

Centralized Accounts

Centralized accounts are typically stored in a directory service like Microsoft's Active Directory (AD) or a generic Lightweight Directory Access Protocol (LDAP) implementation. These are commonly referred to as directory-based accounts. The benefit of centralized accounts is that they allow for a single point of management for all of the subscribing resources that must authenticate against a given account.

A directory-based account may also use entitlements based on policies (authorization) assigned to the specific account or to a set of accounts managed in a group.

Centralized accounts allow users to login into various resources throughout an enterprise and provide access to assets and data in order to perform authorized tasks. This provides the user a single account for multiple purposes and removes the need for a local account in each resource. The risk here is fairly straightforward and somewhat obvious. A compromised central account allows a threat actor to infiltrate and potentially misuse all of the resources associated with that account. If the user is a standard user with basic privileges, the impact is contained, and lateral movement is restricted to just one account and to just one user. However, if the account compromised is a directory-service administrator, or worse a directory-domain administrator, then not only is that user at risk but every other account stored in that directory infrastructure. It is important to remember that centralized accounts can be abstracted to obfuscate account names, but rarely if ever do they have the concept of the one-to-many relationships between an identity and its multiple accounts. This is the responsibility of the Identity Governance system – it performs this layering and linking and supports understanding how threats to an account can escalate to other unrelated accounts and privileges.

Centralized account management is very important for any form of administrative accounts. As a cybersecurity rule of thumb, if a domain administrator account is compromised that includes the domain servers hosting centralized account management, it is game over. Proper mitigation activities would require reloading the entire environment from scratch! Therefore, environments should always protect domain administrator accounts with the highest level of security possible. This should include strong authentication based on multifactor, two-factor, or step-up authentication techniques whenever possible. Every domain administrative account should be unique for any identity that requires domain administrative rights. This practice alone warrants the visibility and management gained by deploying an identity and access management solution.

Functional Accounts

Functional accounts are accounts used to perform automated account management functions. They can be local or centralized, but always have elevated access rights, often domain administrator or root privileges across multiple resources and assets. Functional accounts should always be owned by an identity for control and audit purposes, but they should be strictly used for automation purposes and never be used for any daily work tasks. Ever!

A good functional account architecture limits the reach of each instantiation and prefers multiple functional accounts governing zones, resources, assets, and applications vs. a few that have nearly godlike or domain privileges across the entire environment. This is once again the basic concept of least privilege. These accounts typically also fall outside the remit of any just-in-time management process or privileged access management solution, since they must be considered "always-on." The latter makes it easy to understand that if a functional account is compromised, repercussions are quite pronounced and every account under the functional account's control (managed account) is in jeopardy too. Therefore, in our coffee maker scenario, a functional account would manage all of the accounts of each and every IoT coffee maker. This functional account would then be under the strict control of an Identity Governance solution and its passwords potentially managed inside the PAM solution.

Managed or Proxy Accounts

Managed, or what are often referred to as proxy, accounts have a relationship to functional accounts in that the credentials, or their creation and revocation, are managed by a functional account. Managed accounts can be associated with identities, or they can be strictly electronic in nature. It all depends on the use case. The premise, however, is important. The account is not directly managed by an identity – it is managed through another account type. This distinction can help shield the identity from flaws that would result in duplicate credentials, stale or weak passwords, and other authentication problems that could lead to a compromised identity. This also includes accounts for former employees and contractors that should be disabled or removed.

The entire premise of placing an account under management is to avoid the human element that could introduce increased risk while at the same time providing a vehicle for enhanced security through automation, controls, and the governance of appropriate usage.

Service Accounts

A service account is a special type of local or central account that is created explicitly to provide permissions and privileges operating under an administrative context within the operating system or its supporting infrastructure. The permissions and privileges assigned determine the service account's ability to access local and network resources during its runtime.

The reason service accounts are a special type of account is because they should not have the same characteristics as a person logging on to a system. They should not have interactive user interface privileges nor the capabilities to operate as a normal account or user. Depending on the operating system or infrastructure, this could encompass restricting everything from executing a batch process to not having a proper shell assigned to the account. Service accounts should also not be delegated to any form of just-in-time provisioning model either.

Service accounts should be carefully managed, controlled, and audited, and in most cases they can be associated back to an identity as an owner. Service account credentials can be local or centralized, depending on how they are managed, and in either case can lead to a threat actor owning the process, application, and identity associated with them.

Service accounts associated with identities are typically also associated with machines and other applications with human characteristics.

Application Management Accounts

Application management accounts should not be confused with service accounts. Service accounts provide the runtime credentials required for an application to execute, while application management accounts provide credentials used for applications to interoperate. Think of them as service accounts executing at the application layer only. These accounts are typically referenced in the industry as application-to-application accounts (A2A) and can be found everywhere from integration code to inclusion in operational control scripts and Agile DevOps processes like Chef and Puppet. As another rule of thumb, identities should not be directly associated with these application accounts either. There are really no good use cases to even consider a basic user function being controlled via an application management account. This does not diminish their importance. They too should always have an owner and a controlled lifecycle and runtime. To that end, application accounts exist everywhere in a modern ecosystem and should be subject to the same levels of controls and oversight as every other account.

By definition, if two applications need to share information or interact, they will both need knowledge of the secrets required to authenticate to the application account. This sharing of access can be seen everywhere, from DevOps automation to Robotic Process Automation (RPA). Application accounts must therefore be managed such that any changes to the shared credentials are synchronized between the applications themselves before they are required for authentication. This is typically performed by linking the credentials in an IGA and PAM solution. This allows them to be managed together and to share the same account. This account can of course be a local or centralized depending on the application's implementation.

If a threat actor compromises an application management account, they can impersonate the runtime communications between applications and potentially monitor activity. This can happen by spoofing the authentication process using a man in the middle attack. This has been seen in some of the most famous bank fraud breaches that have been perpetrated over the last few years.

Cloud Accounts

There technically is no accepted definition and terminology to explain cloud accounts. Each cloud provider – Software as a Service (SaaS) vendor, Platform as a Service (PaaS) vendor, and Infrastructure as a Service (IaaS) vendor – uses a different definition to meet their business and technology approaches to solutions and management in the cloud. We are not kidding. Ask a dozen security professionals, and each one will give you a different answer. Therefore, the use of cloud accounts is strictly a vehicle to describe any account in the cloud that is under control of an organization. These accounts may, or may not, have an identity assigned and may or may not have functional, application, or managed account characteristics.

The point of highlighting this account type is that you do not own the environment you are operating in – it is a shared cloud resource. Cloud accounts can have privileges assigned to them, and they may (or may not) support the principles of identity introduced in this book.

A given cloud account may be an administrator, root, or control high-level privilege via some form of role-based access. Although the cloud owner really is the true infrastructure administrator with control over everything from the core application, to the hypervisor to and the network, accounts under subscriber control can still have significant power and privilege. This means you can be compromised in two ways, unlike with an on-premise solution: first from the front – that is, all of your cloud account-based access – and second from the back, everything owned by the cloud provider, including their accounts used to support and manage the service. The latter dynamic is why special considerations need to be made for accounts in the cloud, particularly if they are linked in any way to other identities. And, if the account is a lower-level account used for containers or instances, the attack vector starts at the bottom of the food chain for the threat actor to work their way up into an identity that governs more than just a single instance.

As an example, consider a cloud-based solution that stores biometric information for physical access, transactions, law enforcement, or background checks. Identities linked with biometrics warrant special consideration since you cannot change things like your fingerprints (unlike a password). If this data is stolen from the cloud, portions of the attack vector may be completely out of your control to manage irrespective of the threat actor's attack vector. If successful, the threat actor has a method to authenticate you that can never be changed. This is why protecting cloud accounts is so important. It is the lowest hanging fruit for a threat actor to compromise regardless of any management capabilities you can actually put in place.

Organizations that trust sensitive data and services in the cloud must be aware of the additional risk, and the accounts that safeguard that information should be treated with extra special care. If there is any laxity in procedures and policies for identity, account, password, key, or vulnerability management, the threats cannot be mitigated.

For any cloud service that you trust with your crown jewels, always ask about their security before you subscribe. Ask not only about the security for your access but also how they secure the access from their own employees. Certifications like SOC II/III, SAS 70, SSAE 17, and ISAE 3402 help justify their integrity and will provide some assurance that the risk is being managed for both the providers and your own cloud administration accounts.

Entitlements

Entitlements are any technology implementation that controls access to something we care to manage. Entitlement is a category name used for something that grants, resolves, enforces, revokes, reconciles, and administers fine-grained access, privileges, access rights, permissions, or rules. An entitlement can stand apart from its eventual assignment to an identity and its associated accounts. Its purpose is to define and execute information technology access policy, regardless of resource, asset, device, or application – whether it is running in the cloud, on-premise, or anywhere else. Entitlements come in many shapes and sizes and can usefully be categorized as being either simple or complex in nature – this is explained further in the following. The management of entitlement can be delivered by a range of different technologies and is by convention designed to work across platforms, applications, networks, and devices.

In the Identity Governance process described in Chapter 7, we define how to catalog and manage entitlements of all types as part of a controls and governance process.

Simple Entitlement

Simple entitlements are atomic in nature. What they protect can be infinitely complex and varied, but the entitlement itself is easy to define, provision, audit, and control. A good example of a commonly implemented simple entitlement is a directory group membership being used to control the right to receive IP traffic on my network. "Basic Network Access" is the simple entitlement. It is simple to define – there I just did it. It is easy to provision – I simply put you in a defined AD group, and I can audit and control its use using my deployed identity management solution. What can or can't be accessed once on that network is a far more complex question and in most implementations is the concern of a different more complex entitlement.

Complex Entitlement

Complex entitlements are, well, complex. We meaningfully differentiate them to highlight their complexity in either their definition, their provisioning, their audit, or their control. A good example of a commonly implemented complex entitlement is an SAP R3 role. By its nature, it is a composition of other entitlements (other roles, Tcodes, AuthCodes, etc. – each possibly entitlements in their own right), yet it is assignable as a single unit of access, so it is itself an entitlement.

Controls and Governance

A control (in the context of this book at least) is a clearly defined management oversight function that enables the tracking of adherence to a given security or audit policy. A good example of a control is password policy that states that "all passwords must be at least 24 characters in length." A good example of a DevOps control is the stated requirement that "all logins to the production environment must go through a managed jump-box." In both cases, the control represents a process (and supporting technology) that defines how something must be done to better control security and facilitate oversight.

Governance (again in the context of this book) is the ongoing process of tracking and managing a series of controls, such that there is a known state across many policies. A large part of this book is dedicated to controls and governance over identities and access.

Roles

Roles have been referenced several times already in this publication and have in various ways been critically linked to the various concepts needed for a successful identity access management strategy. At the highest level of abstraction, we define a role as a collection of people, or a collection of access, defined and maintained for the purpose of improved manageability, enhanced controls, and the promotion of good governance.

There are several different approaches to enterprise roles, and for the purpose of this book, we will be describing and advocating for the adoption of a basic two-tier role model. This is depicted in Figure 4-3.

Figure 4-3. *A depiction of a basic two-tier enterprise role model consisting of Business roles and IT roles with managed connecting relationships that support least privilege*

Roles are sometimes used to collect together like identities that perform similar functions and need the same level of access to technology assets. These roles are often referred to as Business roles and are described in more detail in the following. Roles are also sometimes used to collect together related accounts and entitlements required to carry out a known set of actions. These are often referred to as IT roles and are described in more detail in the following.

Business and IT roles are connected together to form user assignment relationships. It's considered a general Identity Governance best practice to only connect IT roles to Business roles and to use the Business role to identity relationship to complete the linkage back to the identity. By employing different types of "connecting relationships" between Business and IT roles, it is possible to further promote the principle of least privilege.

Business Roles

In one sense, Business Roles are simply groupings of people. It is a common best practice to use identity attributes (information about an identity) to filter identities into business role groupings. This is done to simplify managing the entitlement assignment lifecycle. Using organizational information, a business analyst might define a business role to represent a defined dynamic or static population of individuals. By convention and through product implementation rules, business roles have defined business owners and provide a holding place for useful metadata about who, when, and why this business grouping has been defined. Like most group-oriented implementations, business roles support inheritance to enable the creation of hierarchical "trees" of nested roles. Hierarchical business roles provide a useful way to define the "generalization and specification" context required for scalable governance.

The difference between a business role and say a basic directory group comes from where it lives in the ecosystem. A business role is a management abstraction used in the identity management layer only, whereas a directory group is an entitlement construct employed by the target application. Business roles are usually the concern of business analysts, and therefore the technology that implements them must be usable and meaningful to the business users who directly own them and manage their lifecycle.

IT Roles

IT roles are used to collect together groups of like entitlements. As their name suggests, IT roles live in the domain of IT and Information Security and are used to define and manage the specifics of a given security configuration. IT roles "profile" how accounts, entitlements, and permissions must be set in order to meet a given business purpose. Unlike business roles, IT roles do not define how people are collected together. Runtime identity attributes (things like location, age, or authentication type) are often used in the provisioning profiles that make up IT roles, but only to further define a configuration and not to assign the IT roles to a group of identities.

IT roles also support hierarchies and nesting to simplify the definition of complex security configuration, and it is common to find complex encapsulation models in large mature deployments. The goal here is to capture the configuration of entitlement to define a known and managed state. Like business roles, IT technical roles should always have a defined owner, usually someone close to the resource or configuration in question. IT role owners are responsible for managing the lifecycle of the roles they own and are frequently responsible for approving any change to their definition and configuration

Role Relationships to Support Least Privilege

Least privilege can be defined as only giving a user account or processing the entitlement and privileges needed to perform a given intended function. Steering your entire identity, account, and entitlement lifecycle management process toward least privilege will result in better system stability, better overall system security, and a lower overall user access risk profile. Through the careful management of the relationships between Business and IT roles, it is possible to promote and enhance the goals of least privilege.

As discussed, it is considered a general Identity Governance best practice to only connect IT roles to Business roles and to use the business role to identity relationship to complete the linkage back to the identity. By employing different types of "connecting relationships" between Business and IT roles, it is possible to further promote the principles of least privilege. At a minimum, an enterprise-class solution should support mandatory and optional relationships between Business and IT roles. A mandatory relationship says "if you are in this particular business role, you automatically get the entitlements assigned to this set of IT roles." An optional relationship says, "these IT roles are permitted to be associated, but not by default." Giving out less entitlement by default is the ultimate goal of least privilege.

In implementation, optional relationships provide implicit "model-based" control relationships that help guide other processes. For example, in a self-service and delegated provisioning scenario, premodeled optional relationships can be used to "preapprove" a user's request, hence improving user experience while supporting least privilege.

Discovery, Engineering, and Lifecycle Controls

In Chapter 7, we describe in detail how to approach enterprise roles and their discovery, engineering, and lifecycle management. For now, just understand that enterprise role definitions are a critical management control apparatus and need to be secured and managed as such.

CHAPTER 5

Bots

Have you ever asked your home smart device what the weather will be like today or the score of last night's football game? You're not alone. The explosion in virtual assistants in the home environments underscores the reality that software and interactive self-service autonomous consumer applications are now an intricate and interwoven part of our lives.

This explosion in the consumer space is being mirrored in enterprise computing too. Virtual assistants and other autonomous software "bots" are nearing the zenith of their hype-cycle. From customer service chat bots to travel booking assistants, organizations are using bot technology to speed internal processes and enhance the user's experience.

For any organization focused on identity and access management controls, this explosion in the use of bots presents both a potential security challenge and a powerful new controls and management opportunity.

Security Challenges

With the huge increase in the usage of bots, comes new security and business risks. It is critically important that any organization adopting bots for automation consider the implications for security and governance. As these bot-based initiatives gain in deployment numbers, businesses can pave the way to success by employing existing proven models for identity, privilege, and access governance. In practice this means treating bots in the same way that we treat any identity of account that requires access. This often requires building out an inventory and catalog of their presence, purpose, and access requirements. This catalog of bots can then be integrated with the discovery and management capabilities of your identity and access management solution.

Addressing the security challenges introduced by bots also requires the careful and diligent management of their entitlement needs and assignment lifecycle. Any access to privileged information by a bot must be controlled and audited in the same

© Morey J. Haber, Darran Rolls 2020
M. J. Haber and D. Rolls, *Identity Attack Vectors*, https://doi.org/10.1007/978-1-4842-5165-2_5

way that we manage any other access. This management must include full visibility, policy management, and lifecycle controls. Bots must be evaluated against the same governance and privileged accounts access controls as any other account.

Management Opportunities

The wave of bot adoption also provides an opportunity for identity to become more intuitive and pervasive within the business. Not only can bots provide efficiency gains and enhance customer service but they can also be used by the IAM infrastructure itself to facilitate enhanced interaction with the business. This can take the form of chat bots and other forms of more human-like interactions allowing the business users better access to reporting and analytics data.

Users may also become more involved with the actual process of Identity Governance itself. An example of this might be using a bot-facilitated process for access request. This would allow for the process to be further customized to the needs of the end business user. A bot could direct the user to the correct request choice through context and other information at its disposal and thus guide the user to a better result for them and the business.

Governing Bots

The rapid rise in the use of bots throughout most organizations means we all need to take action to prevent this new "aid" requiring a retrospective "Band-Aid." Governing bots from an identity and access management perspective is simple – when the bot is persistent (i.e., a per intent part of the infrastructure), treat it like an identity; when the bot has systems access via accounts and entitlements, manage it just like any other account or entitlement. Cataloging them, understand their context and most importantly control their lifecycle is now a critical part of the overall Identity Governance process.

Most organizations are only now taking their first steps into the world of bots. This affords the identity program staff and planning a chance to get things right from the start. By being proactive, asking the right questions, and using proven governance best practices, we can retain governance and oversight while still allowing for the rapid adoption of this new and interesting technology.

CHAPTER 6

Identity Governance Defined

Identity Governance has emerged as a critical building block in enterprise Information Technology (IT) automation, in enterprise security, and in corporate compliance management. It provides a framework for controlling user access and ultimately helping to reduce overall operational risk. Fortunately, there is a good degree of industry consensus around what Identity Governance means, so for the purpose of this book, we offer the following summary definition:

> *Identity Governance is the technology and processes to ensure that people have appropriate access to applications and systems and that the organization always knows who has access to what, how that access can be used, and if that access conforms to policy.*

Who Has Access to What?

Identity Governance is the process of managing who has access to what. Employees, contractors, and business partners all require access to enterprise systems and data. Understanding **who does** have access, **who should** have access, and how that access is **being used** is a critical business and IT security concern. Figure 6-1 helps illustrate this structure.

© Morey J. Haber, Darran Rolls 2020
M. J. Haber and D. Rolls, *Identity Attack Vectors*, https://doi.org/10.1007/978-1-4842-5165-2_6

Figure 6-1. *Identity Governance is the science of understanding and managing who has access to what across all enterprise data resources*

Understanding **who does have access** is a critical first step in managing the "current state." In order to manage user access, we have to understand how things are set up today. All IT systems have a history. User access comes and goes over time, and without a diligent system of administration and audit, these systems always trend toward entropy and invalid access. Before any level of validation or update can be made to these systems, we have to understand the current state. To provide a useful example, when using Google Maps on your mobile device, before you can get directions to your destination, their system has to know your current location, where you are – your current state.

Deciding **who should have access** is a more complex statement of business security policy, often referred to as the "desired state." Even with an understanding of the *current state*, before we can update or change it in any way, we have to understand what the configuration *should* look like afterward. This means defining business rules and understanding appropriate levels of access in advance. Defining appropriate access is a topic we will come back to many times in this book. For now, simply think of this as your Google Maps destination. When the system knows where you are starting from, and where you want to go – your desired state – the system can provide a clear set of driving directions.

Tracking how access is actually **being used** provides critical input into the overall governance process. All too often, access is provided that is incorrect, unused, or used in an inappropriate manner, and so tracking actual systems usage is key. This process of usage tracking does not imply any breach of user privacy or egregious oversight. It can mean something as simple as monitoring and storing a "last login" date for a given application. Successful best practice shows us that, in order to ensure the ongoing integrity and refinement of the "desired state," we need usage date. Coming back to the Google Maps example, driving directions are greatly enhanced by understanding *current* traffic flows. In today's busy towns and cities, knowing where there is congestion allows mapping systems to provide alternative routes and update recommended directions and estimated time of arrival. The same is true for governance – understanding usage means better controls and more effective security.

Managing the Complexity of User Access

Most organizations today work with a mix of cloud, SaaS, and on-premise systems and applications. Services are delivered through multiple channels and by multiple service providers. Managing access control, regardless of how it is provided to the end user, is the remit of Identity Governance.

User access controls are embedded in our applications, systems, and infrastructure. Each system establishes an access control policy to protect its data. This process of access control often looks simple to those unfamiliar with the process of managing it. People – access – data, how hard can it be (see Figure 6-2)?

People   **Access**   **Data**

Application Accounts   Database Systems   Directory Servers   Operating Systems   PAM Vaults   Access Control   SSO Systems

Figure 6-2. *The complexity of user access control in enterprise systems spanning embedded and externalized methods of control*

It turns out that consistent, comprehensive, and sustainable management of these various forms of access control requires dedicated focus. For even the smallest organization, the implementation of access control ends up being embedded across application accounts, database systems, directories, operating systems, and a range of external access management solutions like Single Sign-On (SSO) and externalized Attribute-Based Access Control (ABAC) services.

Identity Governance solutions help an organization inventory and analyze and understand what access privileges are granted to employees, contractors, and business partners across these various systems. They deliver automation, controls, and governance for all systems of access wherever they reside. Identity Governance provides a high-level management overlay for identities, users, accounts, privileges, entitlement, and access however they are implemented.

The Scope of the Problem

The scope of control required for Identity Governance today is extensive. In cybersecurity, the phrase "you're only as strong as the weakest link" is very relevant here. We have to deliver the right access to the right people across all systems, applications, and data. Automation, controls, and governance are required for cloud and on-premise systems and must span the divide between structured and unstructured data storage systems.

A good example of the importance of scope comes from managing financial data. If, for example, we provide amazing governance over access to our core on-premise SAP system (structured data), yet we allow unrestricted access to a spreadsheet of information (unstructured data), extracted from that system, we have a problem. Today, the adversary understands that file shares and unstructured data resources like SharePoint contain valuable enterprise information. It's our responsibility in Identity Governance to help ensure that controls and oversight are available for these unstructured resources too. We'll come back to the specific challenges around managing these unstructured systems in a later chapter.

Managing the Full Lifecycle of Access

And finally, a comprehensive approach to Identity Governance must address the full lifecycle of user access. We often use the term in Identity Governance "JML" – this stands for **J**oiners, **M**overs, and **L**eavers. This is a phrase taken from the realm of Human Resources and is used to capture the three major states that a typical user access process will go through. Identity Governance is responsible for providing visibility and controls for this full lifecycle.

At each phase of the user's access lifecycle, Identity Governance is responsible for delivering automation and controls to ensure that the right access is maintained – especially when users move between states. We will address how to approach lifecycle management and provide insight into its best practices in the next chapter.

CHAPTER 7

The Identity Governance Process

This chapter provides an overview of the end-to-end Identity Governance process and insights into how best to approach the problem. Later, we will provide an organizational-, project-, and deployment-focused set of recommendations. This chapter is focused on the technology and what to look for when selecting and deploying an enterprise-grade Identity Governance solution.

This chapter lays out the basic steps and major process involved in an Identity Governance (IG) program. It starts with how to establish visibility and context over the current state. It then covers the major elements of an IG process from basic control process to enterprise role management and policy evaluation. We finish this chapter with the advanced process of using AI to create "predictive" governance.

Visibility, Connectivity, and Context

As already discussed in Chapter 4, **visibility** over who has access at any given point in time is a critical first step in the governance process. To manage user access, you have to enable visibility and context over the current access configuration. The phrase "you can't manage what you don't see" has never been more relevant that here. You have to discover everywhere users have access and entitlement via existing accounts and access. In many cases, a given organization may already have a tool that provides some degree of visibility and control over the account management process. You just need to leverage that tool in the initial visibility process.

The critical first part of an overall Identity Governance process is enabling and maintaining visibility over the "current state". This requires integration with authoritative sources of identity, connectivity to target applications where the accounts and access control resides, and the building of something we call an entitlement catalog.

M. J. Haber and D. Rolls, *Identity Attack Vectors*, https://doi.org/10.1007/978-1-4842-5165-2_7

Connectivity to the target resources is a key part of the Identity Governance process. Although there are many ways to implement connectivity, we have always found that the approach to developing, deploying, and maintaining this connectivity is one of the quintessential elements of a successful enterprise-class IGA deployment. Later we provide a comprehensive look at how to approach connectivity and provide a simple classification system for understanding and evaluating how this is done in the Identity Governance solution.

We use the term **context** in the title of this section to represent an understanding of the *meaning* of access. All too often, user access is managed without a good understanding of what that access actually means.

Access control technology, so the accounts, groups, profiles, attributes, and permissions that implement the control inside the target systems, is very rarely developed with the direct interaction of the business in mind. Things like cryptic naming standards and complex hierarchical implementation models make it nearly impossible for non-IT security professionals to understand the context of what the access actually means. "Bob is in the admin group in Active Directory. Does that mean he can access my personal information?" The ultimate goal of Identity Governance is to help answer that question by connecting (or reconnecting) the access security model with the business meaning of that specific access control. Understanding the relationship between identities, users, access, and data is the context we are talking about; creating a consistent map of this access context is one of their primary goals of this technology

Through the process of Identity Governance, we close the gap between the various entitlement control systems and the business users that ultimately own them. As we gain visibility into the various authoritative sources of identity, and we establish application and entitlement source connectivity, we can start to overlay business policies and create the foundation for ongoing lifecycle management.

Authoritative Sources of Identity

Gaining visibility and establishing user access context requires connectivity to all sources of identity across employees, contractors, and business partners. We use the term "authoritative" to mean that these systems are the true source of user records for a given identity type or persona. Unfortunately, these sources of identity information are rarely, if ever, in the same actual application or system. Employee records are fairly consistently centered on a core HR system like Workday or SAP HCM. This is in reference to the employee number we discussed in Chapter 4. Information about nonemployees (contractors, business partners, and customers) tends to be stored in a mix of enterprise repositories like Microsoft Active Directory and custom database application systems. So, in short, identity source records are spread out across multiple systems.

In most organizations, we see multiple sources of identity, even within a given class of users. Due to mergers and acquisitions, system migrations, and the general history of IT, many organizations even have multiple HR systems. A critical part of the IG process is consolidating these various authoritative sources to create a single view of all identity records. This single repository of user data does not replace the original authoritative sources; it simply creates a virtual consolidated view that we often refer to as a "governance system of record." This is that critical linkage between identities and all the accounts they have access to. This governance system of record can then be used as a central point of reference around which we can relate all accounts and access and further apply context.

Approach to Connectivity

An Identity Governance solution should be able to connect to every directory, database, application, and all other repositories of access information – literally every place an identity can be instantiated as an account. An enterprise-grade Identity Governance solution must provide a range of connectivity models in order to meet this goal. These connectors tend to fall into four main categories – these are explained in detail later in this chapter:

- **Direct API** – Using authorized application interface programming calls from a directory source or application, account information can be managed.

- **Shared Repository** – Using a purpose-built repository to share identity and account information.

- **Standards-Based** – Using industry standards for protocols, data sources can exchange identity and account information.

- **Custom Application** – Using custom code or proprietary connectors, identity and account information can be managed.

It should be duly noted that we do not differentiate or classify the connector type by the "cloudy-ness" of the target. Whether the target source is on-premise, in the public/private cloud, or inside the control panel of the Starship Enterprise, it's how you get to that application or system that matters not where its physically located. Be cautious of any identity and access administration system that divides its functionality based on "where the app runs." The end user does not care where the application "runs" and nor should you. An authorized connector that is properly secured should work regardless of where it is placed and what it is connecting too.

Regardless of the classification of the connection type, management, and storage of a connection proxy accounts can be a big issue. For an Identity Governance system to make any form of connection to an external application or system, it requires its own authorization. These are the functional and system accounts defined in another chapter. This is a somewhat circular issue; the governance service manages the end-user credentials in the app, yet it also requires its own account or credential to do so. This access often requires highly privileged API tokens and application accounts. These accounts and credentials must themselves be stored, managed, and audited. As a best practice, we highly recommend the vaulting and management of these credentials in a PAM vault or password safe or API key management system that is external to the Identity Governance engine. We cover the topic of integrating Identity Governance and PAM in detail in a later chapter.

A well-architected approach to connectivity must also allow for things we cannot connect to from the management system. This may sound like an oxymoron, a connector for things you can't connect to, but it turns out to be an important point in the overall approach to visibility and context. To explain, in many systems, it is possible to get "read-only" access to the application entitlement model via a "manual feed." A great example is a CSV (comma-separated values) file provided by a business partner. You don't connect to the application, yet you do have visibility as to its configuration at a given point in time. A standards-based connector (see in the following) can easily import that data and create relevant connections in your identity and account model. But how do you manage and change these records? This is where integrating Identity Governance with an IT Service Management (ITSM) solution becomes critical by providing manual change ticket control processes. By using an internal or external source of "change ticket and tracking," we can still implement a controlled lifecycle for manual administrative changes. This idea of "reading on one channel" (via an export CSV) and "writing on another channel" (via ITSM change ticket) is something we call a *dual-channel approach* and often proves critical to rapid and extensive deployment in the early stages of a project.

Finally, although an approach to connectivity for IG must be comprehensive, secure, and highly adaptable, it cannot be a burden or an anchor to a rapid and extensive deployment project. Therefore, a successful approach to connectivity must also include out-of-box application on-boarding tools that employ "wizards and workflows" and embedded best practices to accelerate the registration and overall entitlement on-boarding process. Look very carefully at these capabilities when designing your implementation and make sure the vendors you consider can do this for every critical application in your environment. Getting the data into the Identity Governance system can be a major hurdle to project success. All vendors, approaches, and technologies are not equal in this area - in fact, you might find some of them extremely limited.

Direct-API Connectivity

Direct-API connectors provide connectivity between the IGA server and the target application by some form or API or remote read and write mechanism. In general, these connectors are provided by the IG vendor and should provide coverage for all of the major enterprise applications on-premise and in the cloud. These connectors typically use the API libraries supplied by the target application vendor and often make use of a stored credential (see the preceding best practice) for authentication.

Examples of direct-API connectors include systems like SAP, Salesforce, Box, Office 365, and AWS (to name but a few). An enterprise-class Identity Governance solution should provide extensive, stable direct-API connectors and must be wholly and completely responsible for managing their development lifecycle across version changes in the target system. That is, they should be forward and backward compatible to older versions that a vendor may have released and easily adaptable to new APIs that deprecate old ones or change functionality.

Shared-Repository Connectivity and Deferred Access

Shared-repository connectors cover centralized systems like enterprise directories (e.g., Active Directory), Single Sign-On systems (e.g., Okta), and all forms of externalized authorization. They are called out here due to the common potential pitfalls with this implementation. To explain, it has been common practice in enterprise application development to centralize application accounts and key parts of the application access to a shared repository like Active Directory or LDAP. In this model, a group membership is used to control functional access inside the application. The access control is therefore deferred (hence the title) from the application to groups and group membership within the centralized service.

In order to audit and administer this class of application access, we must connect to the shared repository. The challenge then becomes sorting out which group membership (entitlement) belongs to which application. It's important to understand that to the directory, these are just accounts and groups, and there is nothing to relate them back to the actual applications. The governance solution must then break out this "one connected resource" and allow the business user to understand the context of the "many applications that it is serving." As an example, let's revisit Bob. He is John Titor's friend. Bob is a user with an account in an admin group; when the admin group is the authorization model for MyCustomApp, we must govern at the MyCustomApp level, not just at the "shared-repository" level. Poor implementation of shared-repository connections can be a significant hindrance to business user adoption and overall deployment success. Look carefully at this issue when selecting and architecting a solution for your environment and pay attention to how each vendor handles these models.

Standards-Based Connectivity

Standards-based connectors cover any form of target system connectivity that can employ (or reuse) a standard connection technology model. Good examples of standards-based connectors are for systems like LDAP, JDBC, CSV, REST, and SCIM. Here the target system supports a standards-based connectivity API. The IG server then simply employs that API and allows for the "registration of new instances" of the application, without the need for any new connector code.

In most cases, standards-based connectors are a special case of direct-API and shared-repository connectors and are only listed as a separate category here due to weaknesses and flaws that may exist in their implementation. For example, target instance registration must be simple and easy to use – a simple matter of inputting a few connection parameters and possibly defining a schema for import. This is often not the case in vendor implementations. In any case, the connector code must be maintained by the vendor, and all aspects of the deployment must be lightly streamlined and wizard-based including authentication to the shared resource.

Another example of an important standards-based connector is the **S**ystem for **C**ross-domain **I**dentity **M**anagement (SCIM RFC-1746). This warrants a special shout-out as a significant standards-based connectivity model. In an ideal world, every application would have full support for SCIM. Later, we will have an expanded discussion of SCIM and its implementation of this important standard.

Custom-Application Connectivity

Custom-application connectors allow for a specific tenant or deployment of the IGA service to develop its own custom connections for target resources not covered elsewhere. Typically, the customer (or its deployment/technology partner) will go through the same process that the Identity Governance vendor did, to deliver its prepacked direct-API connectors or custom protocol connection adapter. For custom-application connectors to be successful in deployment, they should follow important best practices around *development* and *deployment*.

In *development*, custom connectors should be based on a tool kit provided by the vendor. This tool kit should guide the developer through best practices in the development and must provide technology to ensure the testing and integrity of the finished connector. In *deployment*, no custom connector should be able to change or affect the lifecycle of the core underlying governance server or service. This sounds so obvious that the reader may assume this to be the case for all systems. However, this is often not the case. Some implementations of custom connectors can break the overall deployment by affecting the functioning of the "higher-level" components of the IG process (i.e., lifecycle management, certification, or policy controls). And of course, like all other connectors, connector authentication must be secure and resilient – custom or vendor supplied.

Connector Reconciliation and Native Change Detection

An Identity Governance (IG) system is responsible for the administration and configuration management of access control wherever it resides. The connector tier is responsible for reaching out into the infrastructure, making changes, and thus managing accounts associated with an identity or an owner. However, changes often happen locally to that application or infrastructure. Local admin actions can and do happen, and it's the job of the IG system to understand those changes and "do the right thing." This is the process of reconciliation and change detection.

There are two primary methods of understanding that something has changed out in the real world. Either the IG system is notified of the change by the target system, or it does a delta change analysis based on its own cached (previous) version of the configuration – this is traditionally referred to as reconciliation or recon in the IG vendor space. It is important that your IG system and processes support both methods. If available, change detection from the managed system itself is preferable. For example, most LDAP servers support a special attribute polling mechanism (in Microsoft Active Directory, this is referred to as "USN-Changed") that tells the reader that something has changed. This removes the need for the costly processing associated with a delta change assessment by the IG platform.

Historically, reconciliation and change detection have been a significant area of product differentiation. Outside of the processing cost of delta change analysis, some systems do not handle reconciliation well. When the reconciliation process finds delta records, these "badly behaving implementations" have no choice but to treat the local change as an error and automatically change it back to the previous known value. This can cause unforeseen issues with product maintenance, upgrades, and even runtime security. Mature IG systems will allow for change triggers and control processes to be executed upon local change detection. This allows for the execution of business process logic, rather than a blind admin overwrite. Having the ability to "handle the change with a business process" can be a significant factor in initial deployment success when local changes tend to be more prevalent and ongoing change control is less robust.

Correlation and Orphan Accounts

As discussed, the overall goal of an Identity Governance (IG) project is to understand and manage the relationships between people, access, and data. At the core of this goal is the logical connection between an account, token, or credential (the access) and a real human being. The ongoing process of connecting people to accounts and access is called **correlation** and is shown in Figure 7-1. In the ideal world, every account matches up perfectly with a human (identity), and you have 100% correlation (for the record, that's something we never see out of the gate). Account access that does not correlate back to a known user is often referred to as an **orphan account**. Orphan accounts can be a significant security weakness. Post-breach forensic analysis shows that the adversary creates and uses new accounts throughout the cyber killing chain. It is therefore essential for ongoing governance and security to instrument, and, if at all possible, to automate, the detection and rapid resolution of orphan accounts.

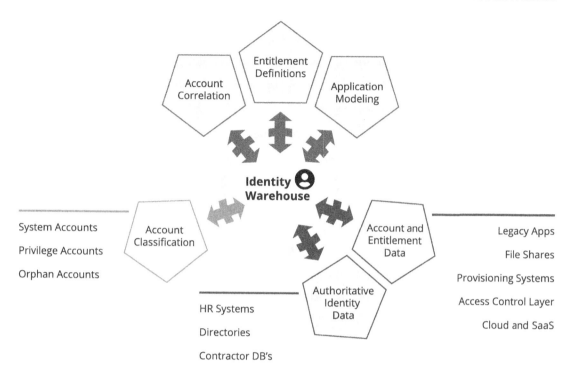

Figure 7-1. *A summary of the overall account and privilege correlation. Identities, accounts, and privileges continually flow into the system, and items that don't connect back to a human are flagged for the attention of application and system administrators*

The presence of system, functional, privileged, and application accounts poses a significant challenge to this process. The accounts and privileges used for system-to-system access and the administration of the IT infrastructure are rarely if ever directly correlatable to a known user without a dedicated process. In large ecosystems, there can be hundreds and potentially thousands of accounts that will not correlate without a deliberate and specific process of managed correlation. An enterprise-grade IG solution will provide core product capabilities to help either manually or automatically resolve these issues. Manual correlation using graphical "searching and connecting" will greatly help the admin establish and maintain links between known owners and orphan accounts. Automated matching algorithms can also help suggest relationships and potential connections. This automated discovery technology can also provide important insights around the integration with Privileged Account Management (PAM) solutions. Finding privilege and directing the PAM solution to take control of the account can be a significant win. Chapter 13 provides more details on the best practices around the integration between PAM and IG solutions.

Visibility for Unstructured Data

As highlighted in the introduction of this chapter, it is critically important that an enterprise Identity Governance (IG) process covers the information and intellectual property stored in files and unstructured data repositories like OneDrive, Box, and SharePoint. Visibility over who has access to what must include this information, so it is increasingly important that we connect, aggregate, and correlate from our unstructured repositories too.

Critical in this visibility process is the ability to inventory, classify, and comprehend what is stored where and how it is protected and actually accessed. The file classification process helps inventory and understand where secrets are stored. Traversing and documenting the access control model for file storage devices and services helps us understand the complexities of its access. All of this information must be integrated with the overall governance process and made available from the enterprise entitlement catalog. Only then can the data classification be mapped back to acceptable use by an identity.

Building an Entitlement Catalog

At the center of the Identity Governance (IG) process sits the entitlement catalog. An entitlement is the generic name given to a technical access control facility that we care to catalog and manage. Whereas an entitlement catalog is simply a registry of these capabilities found across all systems, how this catalog is built, maintained, and leveraged across the IG solution is of critical importance.

The catalog itself provides a place to register entitlements and establish metadata and context on their meaning. We use the term entitlement as an abstraction for all things that provide access. It provides a place to normalize access across the many and varied forms of its implementation. It provides consistency and business level context for the complexity and neuance of access. Enterprise-class IG solutions have sophisticated and extensive capabilities in this area. When selecting a commercial IG solution, we recommend looking for an entitlement catalog that delivers best practices around defining ownership, approval process, definitions, and classification capabilities. The entitlement catalog is the center of an IG solution, so look for a highly extensible metadata framework aspart of the solution. This metadata will allow you to define custom attributes that represent your business's needs and satisfy the business requirements for regulatory compliance.

Later on, we discuss the topic of zero trust and attribute-based access that expands on this metadata concept. A flexible entitlement catalog will greatly help drive the zero trust cause by allowing for the "promotion" of basic identity attributes like "location" or "job code" to be entitlements in the catalog. When identity attributes are used in access control decisions, they become "entitlement giving" and we must manage them as such.

And finally, in advanced systems, look for lifecycle controls over the catalog itself. When access decisions and control processes are based on information stored in the catalog, look for approvals and change controls over the catalog itself. Remember that, in an entitlement-driven control system, metadata is king; so protect your metadata like it is the crown jewel. It literally is the data map for all identity-based entitlements within your entire managed environment.

The Power to Search and Report

In conclusion for the topic of visibility, controls, and connectivity sits the power of search and reporting. Now that we have all this information on people access and data, let's make it available and visible to the people and processes that can benefit from it. Regardless of how the information is being stored inside the Identity Governance (IG) solution, it is critically important that the data is available to search, query, and report upon. An enterprise-class solution will provide multiple paths to access its data. In developing your IG processes, plan for a simple search and query capability that allows business and IT security staff to find people, view their current and desired state access, and, importantly, understand the meaning of this access at a business and data security level. All structured and unstructured query and reporting capabilities should be able to be run at scheduled intervals and be delivered via email with "click-through" verification to confirm, track, and audit their delivery and acceptance.

Lastly, all IG solutions must ensure that reports, queries, and all data access inside the IG solution are fully respectful of a defined security and privacy model. Specifically, this means establishing and maintaining strong access controls over who can access and retrieve data from the IG system at all times, whether from the user interface or from a data access API. This usually requires the IG solution itself to have a complete Role-Based Access Control (RBAC) model of its own in order to meet these requirements. Information is power and we must ensure that the critical information stored inside the IG system is protected at all times.

Full Lifecycle Management

Lifecycle Management (LCM) is at the center of the Identity Governance (IG) process. It captures, models, and maintains the core states of the "automated assignment lifecycle." One of the major objectives of an IG system is to provide controls and automation throughout the ever-changing lifecycle of the user and their access to data. A summary of the overall LCM subsystem is shown in Figure 7-2.

Later in this chapter, we provide insight into how the LCM "state model" usually works and describe the process flows in a typical implementation. At the center of the LCM process are governance models. We will cover what governance models are and describe the pivotal role they play in the overall LCM process. We'll also break out one of those models – the enterprise roles – and provide a more detailed view of the "role" they play in the LCM process. We finish this topic area with a discussion on embedded controls and what to expect in the area of controls automation during the LCM process.

Figure 7-2. *The overall LCM processes. At the center are the core governance models that drive the LCM process. Surrounding these models are the major LCM events and actions that drive the system*

The LCM State Model and Lifecycle Events

The overall goal of a Lifecycle Management (LCM) system is to provide automation and controls for the complete lifecycle of system and application access. We use the term "LCM state model" for the title of this section because at its core, the LCM process is best driven by known states and the transitions between these states called events. In the simplest example, we might model an employee state as being either "hired or fired." When someone receives a terminal letter, we record a "leaver event," and we carry out the actions defined in the governance model for this event – most likely "remove all access." So, at the highest level, an LCM system drives its automation based on known states, change events, and clearly defined governance models.

LCM States

LCM states tend to be centered on the people or users of systems that flow into the LCM model from HR and contractor management sources. Most established HR processes come with their own defined state models; examples from a model system are shown in Table 7-1.

Table 7-1. *Sample LCM states*

Sample LCM States	
Prehire	In many systems, employee and contractor records flow into the IGA system before the users' start date. These user records are modeled as "prehire" to enable the IGA system to carry out actions prior to an official start date.
Hired	When a record moves to the "Hired" LCM state, the system triggers provisioning actions associated with the start of employment or contact.
Terminated	When a record moves to a "Terminated" LCM state, the system triggers actions associated with the removal of access.

An enterprise-class Identity Governance (IG) system should come with a defined set of LCM Human Resources (HR) states out of the box, but will also be configurable to capture the new states specific to each deployment scenario.

Joiner, Mover, and Leaver Events

Although most organizations use a formal HR process with their own "employee record states," it has become common practice in Identity Governance to adopt an abstraction of the main record state and define specific control actions when users join, move, and leave (JML). JML events are often triggered by HR record states, but can also be triggered by the IG system itself. Remember that the primary goal of an IG system is to overlay governance and to provide automation and sustainable controls. Therefore, a JML event could be triggered by an action initiated in the IG system user interface (UI) or may be based on a control threshold being hit like a maximum risk score. In this sense, a JML event is a core governance action rather than a change in HR status, so most automated systems differentiate between the two.

Lifecycle Triggers and Change Detection

Many things can cause trigger actions within an enterprise-class Identity Governance (IG) solution. JML events are a simple abstraction of the broader class of actions often referred to as lifecycle triggers. These events can be triggered based on just about anything inside the IG system or from an external API call. The idea is to "run a process," usually a predefined workflow or program execution hook, based on some change in the access model, its state, or its context. An enterprise-class IG solution will allow for extensive configuration in this area and in doing so will allow for the support of many varied management use cases.

A frequent use of lifecycle triggers is to execute a defined control. You should expect to see the ability to execute standard governance actions such as access reviews, reapprovals, policy evaluations, and standardized workflows when trigger points are met and lifecycle events are executed. You should also expect the configuration and ongoing maintenance of this area of solution to be fully supported in the UI of the product. It is increasingly important that these types of "business rules" are visible to, and under the control of the business user, and not an IT programmer. Having the configuration of triggers and associated actions buried deep inside deployment code should be considered a bad practice.

Often lifecycle triggers are executed based on value changes in the data observed or cached by the Identity Governance system – this is often referred to as change detection. It's important to understand the difference between LCM change detection and connector reconciliation. Here we are creating event triggers based on value changes in governance model rather than in the connector change data. For example, we might choose to post a notification when a "security clearance" attribute changes in a managed application, or we might set the system to re-execute an approval process when there are more than a certain number of changes to an individual user's entitlement assignment state. This "overlaying of controls" is an important part of the value of a governance-based approach to lifecycle management.

Delegation and Manual Events

As depicted in Figure 7-2 on the overall LCM process, an important lifecycle input comes from the UI of the Identity Governance (IG) solution in the form of manual delegation events. A core value proposition of a governance-based approach to identity management is providing a UI for the business to carry out actions and actually take control. This then becomes the interface for day-to-day management actions. Allowing delegated administration over fine-grained access frees the IT security administrator to focus on setting policies rather than executing changes. The ultimate manual delegation is self-service, the delegation of responsibility for a prescribed set of administration actions to the individual end user. This usually includes functions such as access request, password resets (inside or outside of a Single Sign-On solution), account unlocking, and the ability to participate in the ongoing certification and verification of access.

We highlight these manual LCM inputs because they should not happen in isolation. All changes, whether native to the managed application, automated by the IG system, or input from the UI initiated by the end user, *must* be subject to the same controls and governance; all must be fully documented and logged for governance reporting and threat detection.

Taking a Model-Based Approach

At the center of Figure 7-2 are the core governance models that drive the automation process. As we described in the introduction to Identity Governance (IG), it is critically important to establish core policy models that define the desired state. The term "policy" is considerably overused in IT and specifically in the security and management of IT. For the sake of clarity, we offer the following working definition of a governance policy model:

> *IGA policy models are used to capture the desired state, known best practice configuration, and an inventory of controls and governance actions. These models are abstract representations of how accounts and privileges should be set, approved, audited, and used to some known state. Examples of IGA policy models include the entitlement catalog, provisioning schemas, approval and ownership records, audit requirements, role models, lifecycle triggers, and Separation of Duty rules.*

All of the different model record types that are defined and used in the IG process form a baseline for reconciliation between the current and desired state. An enterprise-class IG solution will, wherever possible, provide easy-to-use graphical UI capabilities to make these models accessible to users from the business side of the house. There's a phrase often used around successful IG deployments – it goes something like "let the models drive the process." This simple phrase captures the importance of the models themselves and how they should be employed by the governance platform during the ongoing lifecycle process.

Enterprise Roles as a Governance Policy Model

One of the most often used and most hotly debated governance model is the enterprise role. The "enterprise" prefix is important. There are many types of roles in many different types of systems. Here we are specifically referring to the groups of entitlements and control policies defined and managed in the governance system itself. Enterprise roles (just called roles from here on out) are a critically important model to get right. You don't have to use them to operate a governance-based lifecycle, but if you do use them and you get them right, you can vastly simplify the whole process.

The basic definition of roles was covered in Chapter 4 and will be expanded upon later. For clarity here, simply understand that a good role model will provide a place to define, verify, and reconcile access, a place to define the correct configuration or entitlement, a place to establish assignment approvals, and a place to track the ongoing state of access across potentially thousands of target applications, hundreds of thousands of users, and millions of entitlements.

Embedded Controls

As discussed earlier in this section, regardless of where change input or request comes from, you should never be able to circumvent the governance policy. This is another one of those conversations like functional accounts – where never means never! The term embedded controls is used to highlight the fact that governance policies (like approvals and separation of duty rules) are embedded in the process. We will cover detective and preventive policies later in this chapter, but for now, we simply need to highlight that, throughout the lifecycle of access – from Joiner through Mover to Leaver – controls like Separation of Duty (SoD) - clear approval processes, and specific audit controls like event-based access reviews should be embedded into the governance process.

Provisioning and Fulfillment

Provisioning is the term long used in identity management to represent the overall process of delivering access to applications and data. It usually involves employing various connectivity means to deliver the right access to the right people at the right time. We suffix provisioning with the term "fulfillment" as a reminder that, in complex enterprise scenarios, there are a multitude of ways that this access can be fulfilled. Provisioning and fulfillment (for brevity, here on referred to as just provisioning) in a governance-based approach represents how the system assures completion of an action, regardless of how it gets delivered across the "last mile."

Provisioning Gateways and Legacy Provisioning Processes

As discussed earlier relating to the best practices for connectivity, in governance we must allow for a myriad of ways to connect to the applications and systems that need to be managed. In complex enterprise scenarios, the provisioning server or process may not have routed Internet Protocol (IP) access to the target applications. For example, when applications sit behind corporate firewalls, or are deployed behind Network Address Translation (NAT) subnets, the governance solution may need to provide a gateway process that can provide a single secure inbound connection channel, to marshal the provisioning for multiple target applications running behind that NAT or firewall. In some scenarios, a gateway might be a "dumb router of requests" and may only be used to circumvent network topology restrictions and IP routing limitations. In other scenarios, a gateway might be a sophisticated software appliance that offers guaranteed delivery, enhanced security, and increased performance. In either case, the Identity Governance process uses the gateway as a pass-through fulfillment engine. This provides a basic tiered architecture model where the gateway is the only resource managing the connection between the governance server and the managed resources and assets.

In deployment, it is also commonplace to encounter legacy provisioning systems and processes, either commercial off-the-shelf solutions (COTS) or homegrown custom-engineered processes. In either case, these legacy capabilities will often remain in place for an extended period. It then becomes the job of the new governance-based provisioning platform to deliver a connector to, and for, that legacy system. More advanced Identity Governance platforms will abstract this provisioning integration pattern and create a standardized modular approach that can help drive simpler integration code and promote lower maintenance costs over time.

Provisioning Broker, Retry, and Rollback

An enterprise-class provisioning engine is a sophisticated piece of software. It is responsible for initiating, managing, and monitoring all changes to downstream systems. When a governance platform supports the encapsulation of entitlements into groups and roles, the provisioning engine has to understand the potentially overlapping obligations this can create during the ongoing assignment and de-assignment lifecycle. It is commonplace to find the same entitlement being used in different groups and roles. Therefore, the provisioning logic has to understand a complex matrix of responsibilities and obligations and only add or take away the right attributes and entitlements. This process of "brokering" change across a complex state model and a complex connector model is depicted in Figure 7-3.

Core IGA Policy Models

Provisioning Broker

Connector Framework

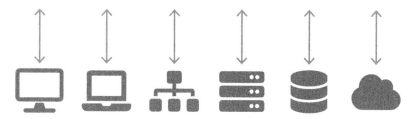

Figure 7-3. *The provisioning "broker" challenge – manage state across competing requests and various connection means*

It is also worth examining how a given provisioning engine executes in fail-over, disaster recovery, and retry scenarios. Target systems will always at some point be "unavailable," and read and write transactions will subsequently fail from time to time. It is therefore critically important that the engine itself is resilient to a host of error conditions. For example, when provisioning an enterprise role that contains four entitlements from four separate systems, if the last of the four provisioning actions fails, should the rest of the entitlements be "rolled back" and removed? Or when a failure does occur, how many times should a failing transaction be retried before the engine just gives up and moves into rollback mode? Answering these questions ends up being both target system specific and use case dependent. It is therefore essential that the provisioning engine should be flexible enough and configurable enough to handle all such scenarios.

An essential part of dealing with the complexity of the enterprise provisioning process comes from its internal management and monitoring capabilities. There are "a lot" of competing things going on in the provisioning tier, so it is essential that the core engine should provide metrics on all aspects of its execution and process flow. If these items get out synchronization due a network outage, natural disaster, or other condition that causes resource unavailability, reconciling multiple changes can be a monumental task. Unless the Identity Governance solution has comprehensive, built-in tracking, monitoring, and root-cause analysis capabilities, managing the provisioning processes themselves can be burdensome.

Entitlement Granularity and Account-Level Provisioning

In some simple implementations of a provisioning process, fulfillment stops at the account level. When the provisioning engine does not understand or profess to manage "entitlement granularity," it is said to support "account-level provisioning" only. These implementations do not understand entitlement granularity and do not manage the account attributes that define the actual access control model. In these scenarios, a separate, often manual process is used to add the actual entitlements to the account out of band.

Our experience shows that, without full scope of control over entitlement granularity in the provisioning process, control gaps soon emerge. Account-level provisioning is a short pour from the enterprise provisioning cup and in our opinion should be avoided wherever possible.

Governance Policy Enforcement

A key part of adopting a governance-based approach to identity is the ongoing development and enforcement of governance policies. Identity Governance (IG) policies form a backbone for operational efficiency, enhanced security, and sustainable compliance. There are many different types of policies and several ways they can be implemented. In this section, we provide an overview of the business rules that drive access compliance and discuss how Identity Governance policies can help. Here we provide an overview of the three main policy types typically seen in an enterprise deployment, and we introduce the differences between detective and preventive policies when used as part of an overall governance-based approach.

Business Rules for Access Compliance

In Chapter 8, we'll discuss meeting compliance mandates. Working with internal and external audit, each business will define its own set of business rules to drive sustainable compliance over user access. The business rules that drive sustainable compliance are just that – business rules – and therefore should ultimately be owned by the business users. For this reason, it is a common best practice for business rules captured in a governance platform to have strong delegated administration capabilities. This allows actual business users to view, edit, understand, or, at the very least, "sign off" on policy definition lifecycles. This delegated administration is how the governance system should be designed to work on a daily basis. Identity Governance should not be the responsibility of just one team "in compliance." Identity Governance business policies span multiple groups and should include multiple participants. Good governance policies should have strong metadata to document ownership responsibly and where possible should also capture remediation advice that is meaningful to the business users dealing with the policy violations it uncovers.

There are many different types of business rules out there. The most commonly deployed policy types we see in deployment are Separation of Duty policies, account policies, and entitlement policies, each of which are described in more detail in the following sections.

Separation of Duty (SoD) Policies

Separation of Duty (or SoD) policies are a common audit requirement in regulated industries. The goal is to identify users that have conflicting access inside the same application (inter-application) or between related applications (intra-application). Based on job roles and responsibilities or relative to inappropriately overlapping personas, SoD rules provide a framework for understanding what should and shouldn't be allowed. In general terms, these policies look to identify any individual that is responsible for completing a sensitive transaction without verification and oversight. The textbook example often used is "invoice creation" and "invoice payment" within the same vendor payment system – sometimes shortened to the "maker-checker problem."

From a security perspective, SoD can be a significant factor in the prevention and detection of infrastructure security issues too. It is common practice to mandate a separation between the development, testing, and deployment of security measures. This can help reduce the risk of unauthorized activity and common configuration mistakes.

Due to the potential complexities involved in defining and implementing SoD rules, it is highly desirable to have an automated system that can help test and simulate SoD rules before they are executed in live situations or placed into live production scenarios. Being able to pre-run and evaluate the violation output *before* any violation events and processes are kicked-off will optimize time for rule development and can help ensure rules are fit for purpose.

Account Policies

It is also commonplace to encounter business policies that affect basic account provisioning. Policies are often required to manage accounts that have not been used for a specific period of time (usually referred to as dormant or stale accounts). Dormant accounts are a known common identity attack vector and are of specific concern to IT security. They also represent wasted resources. With an enterprise Salesforce account costing as much as $3,000 per user per year, it is easy to see how the management of unused accounts could also be a significant cost-savings too. Dormant accounts should not be confused with rogue or phantom accounts which are created to meet objectives outside of accepted business policies.

Account policies can also help manage the overall access risk profile for an organization by tracking people with multiple accounts in the same application or infrastructure. The more access people have, the more damage they can do if their identity becomes compromised. In this sense, tracking accounts-by-identity can provide insight into areas of most exposure and risk and can help ensure that the account correlation and ownership process is adhered to at all times.

Entitlement Policies

As described earlier, a critical part of the governance process is understanding and cataloging your entitlements. This "entitlement context" allows you to build policies that enforce specific assertions about who should and who shouldn't have access to the systems and data we are responsible for. For example, an entitlement policy might look for non-managers with access to manager-specific applications. During organizational changes such as individual promotions and wholesale department reorganizations, people's roles and responsibilities often change, and their actual systems access often does not. Entitlement policies are a useful construct for embedding checks and balances into the change process and making sure that access restrictions are enforced when user responsibilities and organizational alignments change.

Preventive and Detective Policy Enforcement

Preventive policy controls represent an attempt to deter or prevent some undesirable state or event from occurring. We say preventive because they are proactive and stand "in-line" for a given change and prevent it from going the wrong way. You can think of this as being a real-time policy evaluation. Some good examples of preventive controls are separation of duty rules implemented at the time of new access provisioning or self-service access request. Quite simply, don't let bad configurations get setup in the first place.

Detective controls are simply a periodic process to find these same undesirable states once they have already occurred. You can think of this as being a batch-oriented policy evaluation. Good examples here are access reviews, reporting and analysis, and inventory variance assessment. SoD analysis is also relevant here as we still need to check that a "toxic combination" has not occurred in the underlying system without our knowledge or participation.

One of the most common questions that arises from the discussion of preventive and detective control is the statement that "if an organization has full preventive controls, do they still need detective policy evaluation"? The simple answer is you need both. In the perfectly organized world of administration utopia, all changes happen in sequence and according to policy. In the real world of IT and business, things trend heavily toward entropy and errors, and omissions should be expected. The right approach is to strike a balance between preventive and detective policies and ensure that critical checks and balances are done in-line and executed periodically as a safety net.

Violation Management

If you have important policies, you have important violations to those policies. With governance rules touching security, operational efficiency, and compliance, it's increasingly critical to carefully manage policy exceptions and violations. This often requires specific tooling within the Identity Governance platform for managing violations, one that has its own dedicated lifecycle management. This typically includes a registry of violations and a dedicated means of auditing remediation steps and actions that take place as a result of the violation

Certification and Access Reviews

Certification and access reviews are an important part of the Identity Governance process. They enable managers or other responsible delegates to review and verify user access privileges in a consistent and highly auditable way. Building on the policy, role, and risk models established during the governance process, access reviews provide a controlled review point for the current state of user entitlement.

Purpose and Process

An access review is a recurring verification process designed to allow managers (or their delegates) to carry out a "manual" check to ensure that users have the right access to the right systems and data. Born out of corporate and financial audit requirements such as PCI and SOX, the process strives to force the business and IT security to come together to ensure least privilege and appropriate user access.

The Identity Governance server collects fine-grained access or entitlement data from all of its connected systems and formats the information into structured "reports" that can be sent to the appropriate reviewers for verification. Typically, a certification is a collection of access reviews. For example, a Department-level Manager Certification process would include individual access reviews for each manager, and each manager would have a separate review for their staff. This process of review and attestation forms a baseline from which we can assess the current state and manage its change over time.

There are many different types of certification and access review – the most common are shown in Table 7-2.

Table 7-2. *Different types of certification and access review*

Certification Type	Description/Purpose
Manager	Shows a manager the access granted to direct reports to confirm that they have the entitlements they need to do their job but no more than they need
Application owner	Lists all identities and their entitlements related to a specific application so the owner of that application can confirm that all entitlements to the application are appropriate
Entitlement owner	Most useful for managed entitlements owned by an individual; lists accounts with a specific entitlement for the entitlement owner to certify
Advanced	Allows for creation of custom certifications based on groups or populations of users
Role membership	Lists identities connected to specified role(s)
Role composition	Shows assignments or entitlements that are encapsulated within roles (role set reported can be filtered)
Group membership	Lists identities assigned to one or more groups
Group permissions	List the permissions that are granted to a group for selected application(s)

In general, certifications proceed through several phases from initial generation to completion. Figure 7-4 shows the various phases through which a certification will flow.

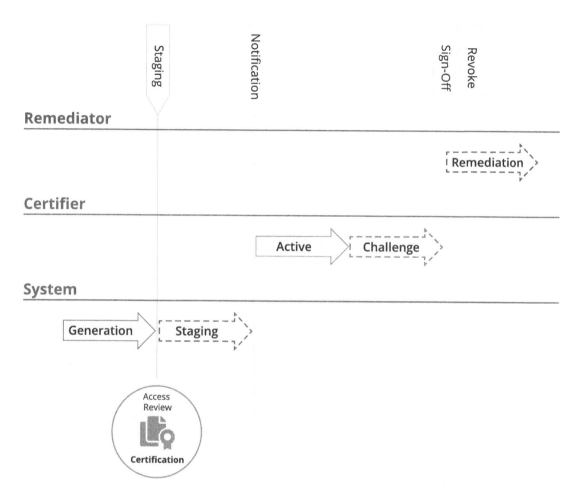

Figure 7-4. *A typical certification process flow*

The first step in the certification lifecycle is the **Generation Phase**. This involves specifying the dataset to be included in the review cycle and defining its schedule. This creates one or more access reviews for the attention of the appropriate certifier(s). The parameters specified for the certification constrain the data to be included in each review and dictate which phases will be applied to the ongoing process.

Enterprise-class solutions will usually provide a **Staging Phase**. Staging allows the system to generate candidate access reviews and "stage" them such that they can be checked before becoming visible to the certifiers. In large-scale certification campaigns, this checkpoint can be a critical operational step in preventing errors and ensuring the best possible business user experience.

Once the access reviews are generated, the next step is the **Notification Phase**. Simply this is letting everyone involved in the process know that they have work to do. Although this may seem obvious and trivial, a certification campaign is often a highly regulated business process, and so ensuring the right people are engaged throughout the process requires various notification means and involves escalations and process changes in real time to ensuring the timely completion of a given campaign.

During the **Active Phase** of a certification, the lines of business are actively reviewing and verifying access. In some cases, it is desirable to have actions and remediations executed in real time with the review. For example, finding that a "terminated employee" still has access to business-sensitive data may require immediate revocation action. In other circumstances, all changes may be collected together into a batch and executed post sign-off of the overall campaign.

Some Identity Governance systems will also implement a **Challenge Phase** in the certification process. Here, identities are notified before a revocation affecting their entitlements is executed; this allows them the opportunity to dispute the decision and offer an argument for why they should retain the access.

The **Sign-Off Phase** is when all of the required decisions have been made for a given access review and the certifier is asked to formally close the review process. Typically, the sign-off action puts the access review into a read-only status that prevents any further changes to the review decisions.

Finally, in the **Revocation Phase**, entitlements are changed in the source applications. Depending on the complexity of the provisioning process and the nature of the connectivity to the target application, the revocation process can be highly manual, fully automated, or a mix of both. For example, if there is no automated provisioning write channel available for a given application, remediation of access in that application may only be practically achieved by sending emails to the admin or opening an IT change ticket.

Certification Pitfalls

The most commonly talked about pitfall in the certification process is the dreaded "rubber stamp syndrome." This is when an approver bulk-approves all access rights by "selecting all" and clicking "approve." Specifically this is done without an understanding of the access, and so no true value-based decision is ever made. This usually happens when campaigns are poorly designed and the appropriate context for the access (business-friendly names, descriptions, metadata, etc.) is not provided to the reviewer.

Certification fatigue can also be a factor in highly regulated environments. When business users feel presented with endless lists of entitlements and with overlapping certification timelines, the reviewers quite rightly get despondent and lose faith in the process. This can all be easily avoided by the proper planning of certification campaigns and by the use of more policy and exception-based approaches to the process. If possible, move to a role-based and delta change–based certification model in an effort to reduce the number of things that need to be reviewed. Most importantly, make sure that the business interface for managing the reviewer process is business-friendly and easy to use.

Another major pitfall for certification is incorrect and incomplete data. The old phrase "garbage in equals garbage out" is very germane here. The access data under review should be as current as possible and the scope of the systems covered as broad as possible. There is little point executing a detective control mechanism like an access review, if the data is wildly out of date or only covers part of the access landscape.

Evolution and Future State

Like everything in the IT space, the process of certification and access reviews has changes as the technology to manage governance has matured. Most enterprises, and most Identity Governance vendors, have been through an evolution in how the certification process is defined and executed. This evolution is depicted in Figure 7-5.

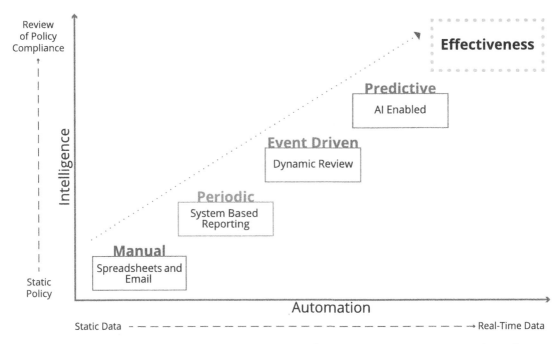

Figure 7-5. *The evolution of certification in which access reviews move from being manual to the future state of an AI-enabled predicative governance process*

In its earliest phases of deployment, the certification process was a **Manual** activity completed with the use of spreadsheets over email. Some organizations still carry out their certifications this way today. If the scale is small enough or the regulatory control mandate "light" enough, this approach may be sufficient. Most organizations, however, quickly outgrow a manual approach; or maybe worse, gaps in the security and integrity of a manual approach make it impossible to meet required levels of compliance.

Many organizations today still approach certification as a **Periodic** control. They run bulk certifications on a regular rolling cadence, and everyone does the "quarterly access review dance." A periodic approach, delivered through a decent user interface that includes current data and informed entitlement context, is more than enough compliance for many organizations. Many Identity Governance vendors also stop here in their product offerings, and this can be a serious limitation for many enterprise environments.

Fortunately, many organizations today are moving rapidly toward an **event-driven** approach to certifications. With large volumes of entitlement certifications to contend with, and a significant volume of data changes in the infrastructure, it's often beneficial to allow lifecycle events and governance policies to trigger dynamic access reviews only when they are needed. For example, you might elect to review all administration rights for a group of admins on a quarterly basis, but then based on unusual admin activity, you might automatically rereview a specific admin. Connecting the ongoing access review cycle to key security "stimulus" can make an access review the very control that stops a breach or exploitation. This then makes an access review one of the basic tools for protecting against identity attack vectors.

The future of certification, however, lies in a **Predictive** approach. Later, we will fully address the topic of Artificial Intelligence and Machine Learning. This technology is enabling next-generation Identity Governance platforms to take the notions of event-driven certification to the next level. Here we see the governance platform making value- and data-based decisions (based on behavioral baseline and peer-group analysis) to create a more dynamic and real-time approach to the process. Imagine your manager being asked to confirm your account groups for a mission-critical application, because you just logged in from an odd location – that's a responsive and highly predictive approach to a detective governance control and is rapidly becoming one of the key future drivers for leading technology providers in this space.

Enterprise Role Management

The topic of enterprise role management could be a book of its own. We only covered a brief definition of it in Chapter 4. In this section, we can still only hope to scratch the surface of this complex and sometimes overwhelming topic. Over the past several decades, roles and Role-Based Access Controls (RBACs) have swung in and out of favor like a giant regulatory pendulum. Throughout this time, there has however always been a thread of inevitable need and vital functional capability that enterprise roles have provided.

Generally speaking, RBAC is an approach to access security that relies on a person's role within an organization to determine what access they should have. A role is a collection of entitlements each user receives when they are assigned to that role. One of the main goals of a role-based system is to grant employees only the access they need to do their jobs and to prevent them from having access that is not appropriate to their persona or responsibilities. A well-designed RBAC system also simplifies and streamlines the administration of access, by grouping sets of access in a logical and intuitive way. Based on things like department, job function, title, persona or region, roles are assigned to users, and their access rights are then automatically aligned with those roles out in the infrastructure. This provides a secure and efficient way of managing access and helps keep things simple for administrators, certifiers, and the users requesting access.

In this section, we will try to focus on the core value propositions for roles and highlight some of the known best practices for their use and overall management. We provide an overview of the current engineering, discovery, and peer-group analysis process and highlight some of the best approaches to the "role definition" process. We then provide an introduction to the topic of managing the lifecycle of these role definitions – so how best to manage the role models you create as the business needs change. We then finish this section with a summary on where we see roles as part of the overall Identity Governance process looking forward.

Why Roles?

When done right, enterprise roles offer a significant increase in operational efficiency for IT audit and for the business user. Today, the business is tasked with owning and operating much of the data access process, and *enterprise roles* (from here on out just referred to as ***roles***) offer a mechanism for simplifying that process. Roles also allow an organization to meaningfully move toward a "manage by exception" paradigm by defining known groups of access aligned with business activities and functions and highlighting where the current state differs from the model view.

Quite simply, roles make certification and access reviews simpler, faster, and more business-friendly. During the business certification process, roles allow the user to focus on the assignment of groups of entitlements rather than getting lost in individual entitlement configuration. This is often referred to a role assignment certification. A separate process can then focus on the composition of a given role – so what's in the role ready to be assigned to an individual – this is often referred to as a role composition certification.

Roles enable a structured control model for the lifecycle of entitlement changes. Imagine needing to add a new application access profile for all "basic users." Roles help prevent having to manage these changes at an individual user or account level. Instead, changes to the access assignment model can be made at the role level and pushed out to each user by the provisioning process in an automated fashion.

Roles also greatly enhance the security audit and controls process. Auditors and security professionals can validate access and access management processes at the role level, rather than working with individual entitlements and individual assignments. This vastly simplifies the administration and oversight burden and allows specialists to focus on defining and validating governance policies instead.

Finally, roles provide an important "model construct." A role (and its supporting metadata and control processes) provides a concrete model construct around which the business and IT can come together to define, capture, and enforce "the desired state," hence helping to ensure that the right people have the right access to the right data.

Role Model Basics

There are many varied approaches to how role models are defined. One of the more commonly employed approaches is to adopt a basic two-tier model to facilitate matching a user's business responsibilities (persona and actual job) to their function access. This is depicted in Figure 7-6.

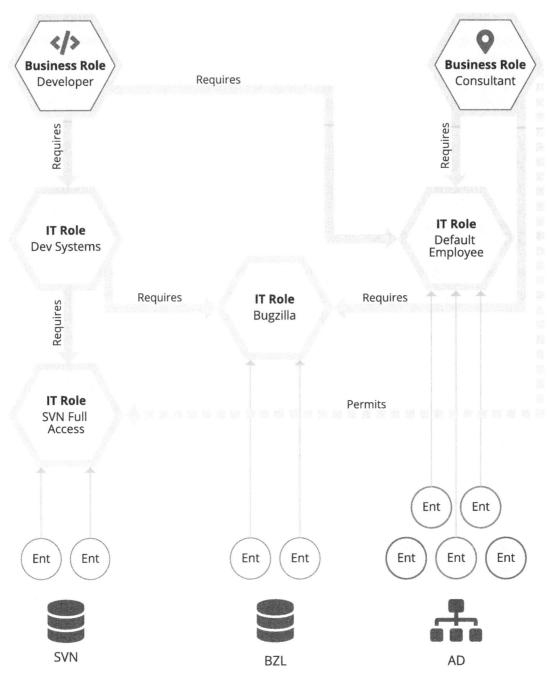

Figure 7-6. *Depiction of a classic two-tier role model with role optional and mandatory assignment relationships*

Business Roles

Generally, a business role represents job functions, titles, persona, or responsibilities. They are usually tied to the organizational structure and are assigned to users based on their functions in the business – such as "treasury analyst" or "accounts payable clerk." Business roles are abstract, logical grouping of people that should share similar access entitlements. They are directly assigned to users automatically via identity attribute matching rules on the role definition – so using an identity attribute like job title or department to collect groups of identities together based on who they are and what they do.

IT Roles

IT roles encapsulate sets of system entitlements. They are tied to actual permissions (which may contain privileged access) within an application or target system. They represent the *actual state* of the user's access, such as an account, an entitlement, or set of permissions required to execute a given function. A user's IT roles can be "detected" by the governance platform based on the observation of the entitlements that the user actually has during account discovery and aggregation. A good example of a detected role would be a "sales engineer" that has access that looks like a "developer" – he or she appears to have the same entitlements as the "basic developer access" IT role, but they have never been assigned that actual role. This "matching" ability can be very useful in the complex world of enterprise entitlement.

IT roles are typically connected back to the identity via role relationships and provisioned to a group of users via its association with an established business role. Here our "basic developer access" IT role contains all the access required for code development, test, and check-in, and it is "assigned" to the "OT Developers" business role members via either a required or optional role relationship.

Required or Mandatory Role Relationships

Required relationships refer to the set of access that someone with a given role must have. Someone with an accounts payable business role, for example, will always need to have read and write access to the accounting system. The required relationship is defined by the relationship type that links together the business role and the IT role that contains the entitlement definitions.

Optional or Permitted Role Relationships

Permitted relationships refer to the set of access that is discretionary. These are groups of permissions or entitlements that a user may be allowed to have, but isn't required to have. When optional relationships are used to connect an IT role to a business role, the entitlements defined in that IT role are essentially "prescreened" – we know that a user with this business role is allowed to have the permitted access. For example, perhaps all employees are allowed to have VPN access, but aren't automatically given this access unless they or their manager requests it. This type of discretionary access can really help prevent the over-assignment of entitlements. It creates what can be thought of as "model-based least privilege" and can really help business and IT teams work together to better understand the lifecycle of access.

Engineering, Discovery, and Analysis

The term "engineering" is used around role discovery and definition for a good reason. When used appropriately, roles form a critical part of the overall governance process. Defining and validating a role really is an engineering exercise and an ongoing process, one that takes skilled practitioners, smart tools, and reliable infrastructure. An effective governance platform will provide a range of tools to help with the discovery and analysis process, but will always be dependent on a skilled staff and solid understanding of the applications, network, and infrastructure environment in question. The tools required include but are not limited to

- **Entitlement Analysis and Search** – A frequently employed starting point for a role engineering project is entitlement analysis and search. With access to an entitlement catalog (showing entitlement context and meaning), and a holistic picture of the current state (via aggregation and the creation of the identity warehouse), the role engineer can carry out ad hoc searches and queries. Simply being able to "see" the data and share that with the engaged business participants can be a big help to the overall role engineering process.

- **Automated Role Mining** – Role mining analyzes data discovered and collected together in the Identity Governance system. It uses pattern-matching algorithms and peer-group analysis techniques to look for collections of, similar, access and outliers. You can use the results of role mining to help determine what new roles to create. In a two-tier role system, the Identity Governance platform should support automated role mining to create both Business and IT roles. Business roles typically model how users are grouped by business function, including functional hierarchies, project teams, or geographic location. IT roles typically model how application entitlements (or permissions) are logically grouped for streamlined access.

- Business role mining facilitates the creation of organizational groupings based on identity attributes, for example, department, cost center, or job title. Business role mining should support multiple configuration options to assist users in generating new roles. After the mining process is completed, the new roles are added to the system for lifecycle management.

- **Peer-Groups and Identity Graphs** – Peer-group analysis is an enhanced derivative of the classic discovery methodologies that is focused on building peer-group data graphs and leveraging a broader dataset that often includes actual usage data. Later, we will discuss more on the topic of peer-groups and data graphs for role lifecycle.

- **Manual Role Creation** – Many businesses still like to use manual methods in the creation of roles. This classic "pen and paper" exercise involves business analysis techniques to help map out commonalities in the access model. It is therefore important that the Identity Governance systems provide an easy-to-use graphical way for roles to be input into the system "by hand" or in a batch based on some form of role import facility.

Role Lifecycle Management

If you are using enterprise roles, you must manage their lifecycle and control their integrity. If the role defines the access, then you must manage that definition over time and across domains. Role definitions need to be carefully maintained and revalidated on a known control cycle. A sage security practitioner once said, "Control the security configuration or be controlled by the adversary." Here, this means regular role composition recertification, tight change control, and version management for business and IT role definitions.

Good management over enterprise roles starts with an understanding of authority. Understanding role authority means having a clear definition of ownership. In practice, this simply means having things like "role owner" metadata in the model – but it also expands to more complex things like restricting role import and "sharing." We often see cases of an Identity Governance system being responsible for "full assignment lifecycle and governance" when the full "role model definition" is delegated to an external unrelated system. If you don't own the model, you don't own the integrity. Therefore, make sure your model is governed by your IG system and not something else. Yes, it is that simple, but yet that important.

Enterprise Role Tips and Tricks

Successfully deploying roles as part of an Identity Governance project can be tough. It's easy to play role quarterback from the comfort of an author's armchair.[1] In reality, however, roles are an area of Identity Governance that warrants seeking help and consultation from an experienced practitioner. That said, here are some best practices that can help any skilled IT or business professional design and implement a successful enterprise role solution:

- **Take a Pragmatic Approach** – Think of enterprise role engineering as an ongoing program, not a project. Don't expect to achieve 100% coverage right out of the gate. A comprehensive role solution could take months, or even years, to complete. It is realistic and acceptable to implement roles in incremental steps or phases starting with areas of the business that see high staff turnover *and* simple user access requirement. Start here and gain experience along the way.

- **Know What You're Trying to Accomplish** – Are you trying to make certifications easier? If so, your primary focus will be on evaluating and modeling current access. Is your goal to make access requests easier? In that case, you may want to focus on using roles to help users more easily find and select the roles they want to request. Define clearly what you are trying to accomplish and why.

---

[1]We had a lot of fun collaborating on this book, as we are both quarterbacks for our respective disciplines.

- **Look for Groupings of Role Types** – Use automated Business and IT role mining and entitlement analysis techniques to identify patterns and groupings of access that can easily be captured and modeled as roles.

- **Enforce Least Privilege** – Define roles so that you don't give people access they don't need. Setting up roles with support for least privilege is a best practice for reducing security risk, both from malicious intent and from user errors. This will form the basis for preventing against privileged attack vectors.

- **Expect Exceptions** – In most enterprises, it is difficult or impossible to entirely avoid individual entitlement assignments, especially in areas of highly specialized access needs, such as an IT department. Don't assume you have to force all entitlements and all access models into the role paradigm.

- **Make Roles Reusable** – If only one person in the whole organization is assigned a particular role, maybe that access shouldn't be managed via a role at all. Make sure the roles you define are applicable to groups of people. Avoiding "role explosion" requires setting carefully engineering limits to the coverage and assignment of roles. Having a small, well-controlled, and extensively used role model is far better than a behemoth that no one understands or uses.

- **Involve the Business Experts** – People within your organization who know the business are often the best resource to engage in both the business role and IT role discovery process. They are often the people that understand access patterns are and how your role model should be used.

- **Test and Verify Your Roles** – Roles need as much testing and verification as any mission-critical application – maybe more. If you define roles suboptimally at the outset and put them into production, you can end up with a lot of users who lack the access they need or who have more access than they should. This can cause a big cleanup effort if you roll out a role structure that has not been set up and tested properly.

- **Develop Processes for Role Maintenance** – Roles evolve, and you need to keep them up-to-date. Plan for periodic review and certification of your roles to make sure they're still current and accurate. Regular certification of role composition and role membership should be part of your ongoing program strategy. This should include a plan for how to retire roles when they are no longer needed. It is important to keep your role definitions accurate and up-to-date, or you can set yourself up to be the victim of the very identity attack vectors discussed in this book.

The Future of Roles

As systems and data access continues to proliferate and decentralize, we find ourselves increasingly dependent on understanding the similarities between people and looking for outliers. A traditional role model is an expression of "expected access," across a known group of users (peers or even personas). The outliers are the entitlements and the people that fall outside of that group. Traditionally, the focus of roles has been the "norms" rather than the outliers. This traditional, somewhat static view of the world is therefore greatly enhanced by an understanding of usage information and a more dynamic runtime connected dataset.

We see the future of enterprise roles enhanced by the construction of "identity graphs" that represent relationships across identity, access, and usage information calculated as vectors. Using peer-group analysis and a range of graph algorithms, we can model scoped populations and carry out a far more granular and dynamic outlier analysis process. This process then results in essential new input into the role modeling process and forms the basis for a more predictive overall approach to the governance process. This significantly enhances the future of role engineering and lifecycle management and is the focus of leading vendors in the enterprise role space.

Governing Unstructured Data

An area of growing importance in the Identity Governance space is gaining control over unstructured data. Of course, everyone understands what data is, but what exactly do we mean by unstructured data? The term "unstructured" refers to the fact that this data has no predictable form or structure – for example, a PDF file, containing personally identifiable information (PII), sitting on a file system or out on a Dropbox share. This data often resides under the corporate governance radar and has an access control model that is usually not synchronized with application-level governance controls and oversight.

Changing Problem Scope

The sheer volume of file-based unstructured data is staggering. Within a given organization, there might be hundreds of thousands, if not millions, of unstructured data items. Is this data sufficiently categorized, monitored, and controlled? Are the effective access models often used for unstructured data understood by security administration staff, and can they be managed in unison with the rest of the access we give to our user populations? Probably not.

The truth is most organizations lack the infrastructure and best practices to properly deal with unstructured data. Many lack the tools to create visibility – to locate, classify, and catalog unstructured data. Most lack the controls to define stakeholder ownership and manage its lifecycle. Few have the tools to define and maintain compliance, and unfortunately, most lack the ability to carry out remediation when security issues are identified. This is a problem an enterprise-class Identity Governance solution can help address.

File Access Governance Capabilities

Some enterprise-class identity management solutions now provide a full suite of management capabilities for applying governance to files containing sensitive information. Table 7-3 highlights some of the governance capabilities required by most organizations.

Table 7-3. *Governance capabilities required by organizations*

Capability	Use/Benefit
Data discovery and classification	Discover sensitive data based on keywords, wildcards, regular expressions, and metadata and how files are accessed by users.
Permission analysis	Evaluate user access to data and how it was granted. Analysis shows access models and ineffective or overexposed. permissions
Behavioral analysis	Classify folders based on the groups or departments accessing the data.
Data ownership elections	Employ workflow and business process flow technology to accurately identify and elect proper data owners by enlisting input from users of the data.
Compliance policies	Predefined policies are designed to accelerate readiness with PII-/PHI-related compliance requirements such as GDPR and HIPAA.
Data access request	Enable data owners to more intelligently respond to data access requests with enriched identity context.
Data access certification	Effectively and accurately respond to audits with automated access reviews and certifications.
Real-time activity monitoring	Track user activity for greater security insight. Monitor access policy violations in real time with automated alerts and responses.

These capabilities are now becoming foundational requirements for most Identity Governance programs. They should be delivered as simple extensions to the broader Identity and Access Governance platform and deployment. The right approach is to bring together the worlds of structured and unstructured access, to create a single holistic approach. This enables the delivery of a single lifecycle control process for both structured and unstructured data. This will enable you to better meet compliance objectives and ensure an identity attack vector does not affect potentially sensitive information from your organization.

Self-Service and Delegation

Self-service and delegation are a major part of the overall business value for an Identity Governance program. Intelligent self-service provides big benefits for business cost management, security process improvement, and end-user satisfaction. For the end user, the smartphone has quite literally rewired how people think about getting services. Everyone now expects to find a catalog of enterprise self-service items and a "push-button" delivery model. From a pure cost management perspective, self-service generally means lower overall Total Cost of Ownership (TCO), so it's a recognized business best practice to lead with a self-service approach in a modern IT environment.

Under the Identity Management governance umbrella, there are now a set of clearly recognized lifecycle management functions that are oriented toward self-service first. In this section, we address where and how Identity Governance self-service fits in the more general IT self-service delivery strategy. Setting a clear direction for the integration between Identity Governance and Information Technology Service Management (ITSM) is an important part of program success. Here, we explain the major options for this integration and make some best practice recommendations. We then finish this section with a deeper dive into the major Identity Governance self-service items of access request, password management, and account controls.

Integrating ITSM and IGA Self-Service

It helps to start this discussion with a formal definition of self-service. The market-leading ITSM provider ServiceNow defines self-service as follows:

> *Self-service is the ability of a service consumer to resolve their issues and needs without having to call support. Self-service solutions can include everything from using simple FAQ pages, knowledge base articles, and the Service Catalog to complex human-like chat sessions.*[2]

That's a pretty big self-service picture, so the important question is, where does little-ol' logical access request and service provisioning fit? Are all of the IAM self-service items just more stuff in a single global ITSM catalog, or is logical access something that should stand-alone? Sadly, there is no simple single answer to this question. Individual

---

[2]www.servicenow.com/content/dam/servicenow-assets/public/en-us/doc-type/bp/improve-self-service.pdf

business drivers, different product capabilities, and the long tail of legacy IT history result in each organization drawing the line between Identity Governance and ITSM at a different point in the stack – these options are outlined here:

- **Launch-in-Context Integration** – In the early days of integrating Identity Governance and ITSM, there was a trend toward a basic launch-in-context approach. This meant putting a single service item (the formal Information Technology Information Library (ITIL) term for something exposed as a self-service thing) into the ITSM catalog for "logical access." Vendor-provided integration then launched the self-service requestor into the user interface of the Identity Governance platform (in a frame or a window). Hopefully this integration also provided the context of a Single Sign-On (SSO) session and deep linking into the service catalog of the Identity Governance product.

  The benefits here are simplicity and the ability for both products to progress on their own lifecycle. It's accurate to call this integration model "loosely coupled," but it's far from reasonable to call it "highly cohesive." Challenges invariably come from a lack of visibility between the two platforms. Even with the best efforts of cooperating vendors, the user paradigm shift and lack of true integration ultimately lead to gaps in visibility and functionality.

- **Pass-Through Fulfillment** – We have also seen a number of successful Identity Governance and ITSM integrations based on a complete pass-through model. Here, a core set of high-value access provisioning services are made "first-class" service items in the ITSM platform, and the governance service is literally plumbed in as an unquestioning and ever-faithful fulfillment execution engine. A pass-through model usually means all the approval action and all the controls lie in the ITSM product scope, and it's usual to see the Identity Governance provisioning fulfillment happen without workflow or any form of interactive approval in that system.

The benefits here lie largely on the ITSM side as it retains full approval visibility. This integration model works well for exposing a small number of very well-defined services – often password reset and a small handful of new access provisioning actions. The challenges here come from a lack of scope (a small number of service items) and the uncomfortable fact that having pass-through provisioning sort of violates the very purpose of having a single control point in Identity Governance in the first place.

- **Dynamic Catalog Integration** – As API and integration capabilities have advanced, a more detailed and comprehensive integration model now exists between some vendors in this space. Here a dynamic exchange of catalog items, approval processes, and fulfillment progress happens in real time. The Identity Governance team builds "requestable units" and marks them for publication in the ITSM catalog. A "requestable unit" has a carefully managed composition and set of fulfillment steps, defined ownership, known approval steps, and a complete set of tracking metadata that drives the fulfillment process both sides of the integration. Synchronization technology then makes the requestable units available as individual service items in the ITSM system, and both sides are able to track the progress of requests as they move from approvals through to fulfillment.

Obviously, this is a fully featured integration paradigm. It benefits from operational integrity and a more dynamic and comprehensive integration model. Unfortunately, this level of integration is only provided by a small number of collaborating vendors and usually does not come cheap.

Self-Service Access Request

Self-service and delegated access request is a basic requirement for most Identity Governance programs. When the business user needs access to a new application or service, they go to their identity and access service portal and search for the access they need. Items are usually added to some form of shopping cart user interface, and after appropriate approvals and controls are completed, the service access is automatically provisioned. There are important nuances to this simple sounding process; these are discussed as follows:

- **Managing Requestable Units** – Inside a large corporate ecosystem, there can be hundreds of thousands of requestable services or units. We define a **requestable unit** as a service item with a well-known set of access entitlements and fulfillment requirements. Sometimes, these requestable units are large buckets of access encapsulated in an enterprise role definition. Other times, a requestable service might be an individual entitlement like membership of a specific Active Directory group or access to a single data permission on a managed file share. Each "requestable unit" is carefully cataloged in the Identity Governance system and has established fulfillment obligations, defined approval processes, and established preventive control definitions and (maybe most importantly) has been assigned the correct business metadata such that it is meaningful to the requesting population.

  It is the specific responsibility of the Identity Governance platform to publish and maintain these requestable units over the lifecycle of the system. Someone has to manage their composition and fulfillment structure and ensure that the defined controls (ownership approval, policy checks, and tracking metadata) are correct and up-to-date.

- Searching and Peer-Group Recommendations – Finding the right thing to request can be a challenge. An enterprise-class governance platform will provide extensive filtering and searching capabilities to help. Allowing the end user (or their delegate) to find services by searching on application, entitlement, and data metadata (so data about the data) is expected functionality.

  Providing peer-group searching and automated recommendations is becoming a key Identity Governance requirement. By leveraging artificial intelligence and machine learning algorithms, a next-generation governance platform can provide real-time awareness to the access request process. Allowing the people asking for things to "see" what others already have, or are asking for, provides key user insight and enables enhanced controls. Understanding "outlier" requests or suggesting likely peer-group entitlement recommendations vastly simplifies the request experience and allows for more dynamic preventive controls to be defined and implemented.

- **Delegation, Capabilities, and Scope** – It is also wise to pay special attention to scope and delegation capabilities for access request. An important part of the operational efficiency gains for an Identity Governance program comes from allowing delegates (i.e., business people, managers, HR operatives, project owners, and the help desk) to make requests for a defined group of people.

  In order to support a secure and auditable approach to access request, the governance platform must provide extensive delegation and scoping capabilities. Requestable units should be scoped such that only defined groups of delegates (or individuals) can see and request them. The overall request catalog model must be flexible enough to allow for complex delegation hierarchies to be defined that only give the right request capabilities to the right people. This is how you allow a project owner in the line of business to be responsible for assigning sensitive fine-grained privileges, in a controlled and auditable manner.

- **Overlaying Data-Driven Controls and Governance** – Approval workflows are the currency of governance. It's critical that the access request catalog is supported by dynamic and data-driven approval processes. This means approval workflows should be driven by metadata on the requestable units and the applications and embedded in the delegation model, and not hard-coded in the approval workflow code. This sounds like a technical nuance, but experience shows that getting this right can be the single most impactful factor affecting the long-term cost and maintenance of the Identity Governance system as a whole.

- As discussed earlier, preventive policy enforcement is a core tenet of access request. Enforcing Separation of Duty controls at the time of access request should be considered a base requirement. As identity-centric artificial intelligence solutions develop to support the access request process, these tools can also provide dynamic peer-group analysis to help overlay more real-time controls that are based on behavioral norms and access request baselines.

- **Request Tracking and Management** – Finally, as is often the case in systems management, visibility is key. The overall access request process must be rich with monitoring and tracking and must deliver meaningful metrics. The system has to provide embedded instrumentation such that everyone concerned can, where appropriate, get full visibility into what's being requested by whom and where these requests sit in the overall fulfillment process. This tracking and management data can be used for detailed reporting on service usage and also provides essential input into the ongoing tuning of service definitions (requestable units) over time. Improper reporting or access awarded to the wrong individual is considered another identity attack vector and potential cause of insider threat and risk.

Password Management and Account Self-Service

Anyone with an online account understands the value of password management and account self-service. Who hasn't forgotten their password or been locked out of their account at some point? Being able to securely reset your own password or unlock your account is a critical enhancement to the end-user experience. A successful password management solution improves business agility and radically reduces operational cost. Industry analysts still estimate that 40% of all IT service desks requests are still tied to password change requests. And, if something as simple as your mailbox is compromised by a threat actor without using multifactor authentication (MFA), a simple "forgot password" request could allow one account to take over your entire identity simply by clicking "forgot password." This can be a significant identity attack vector. Providing secure, reliable password recovery capabilities can mitigate this risk by overlaying controls, governance, and oversight for the process.

To that end, the first generation of password management solutions incorrectly focused on the technical aspects of synchronizing passwords across different systems, rather than the strategic needs of the business user. A modern password management approach provides fully automated password recovery and reset capabilities that leverage extensive out-of-box password policy best practices and extensive multifactor authentication capabilities.

As more business applications and systems move to the cloud, organizations need to extend their existing processes and technology to maintain compliance and security over all systems and applications. An enterprise-class password management service empowers all users – including employees, partners, contractors, and vendors – with a secure self-service platform for unlocking accounts and resetting passwords in cloud, SaaS, and on-premise applications and systems. Obviously, this must be done in a highly secure fashion and must not rely on the simple techniques of selecting "forgot password" and sending an email or text message. Both have been proven to be highly susceptible to spoofing and other attack vectors.

CHAPTER 8

Meeting Regulatory Compliance Mandates

Organizations must approach regulatory compliance requirements with sustainability in mind if they are to manage their risk effectively. This is a security-driven compliance approach, and if we are compliant, we are secure. Security must be sustained in order to be secure. If you do nothing more than what's necessary to pass a SOX or FISMA audit, you are not likely to address your logical access risks or security requirements. Effectively managing user access risk requires meaningful diligence above and beyond "checkbox" compliance. Achieving a sustainable level of transparency and risk management helps to protect against the very real security threats that exist inside the organization should be the goal.

Shown in Table 8-1 are common compliance requirements for organizations based in the United States. The intent of these mandates is to prevent breaches, fraud, and negligent behavior that violates an organization's security.

© Morey J. Haber, Darran Rolls 2020
M. J. Haber and D. Rolls, *Identity Attack Vectors*, https://doi.org/10.1007/978-1-4842-5165-2_8

Table 8-1. *Common compliance requirements for organizations based in the United States*

Regulation	Organizations Affected	Focus	Information Security Requirements
Sarbanes-Oxley Act (SOX)	All public companies traded on US exchanges (including international companies)	Information integrity	Ensure the accuracy of financial information and the reliability of systems that generate it. Section 404 requires management to assess internal controls and obtain attestation from external auditors annually.
Security Management Act (FISMA)	Federal agencies and affiliates	Information integrity	Develop, document, and implement programs to secure data and information systems supporting agency operations and assets.
General Data Protection Regulation (GDPR)	All organizations who conduct business in the European Union	Privacy	Protect consumer data from theft and fraud. Notify all involved parties when a breach occurs within 72 hours and "forget" customer data when requested.
Payment Card Industry (PCI) Data Security Standard	All members, service providers, and merchants that store, process, or transmit cardholder data	Fraud prevention, privacy	Meet 14 information security requirements in areas such as data protection, access control, monitoring, and intrusion protection.
Health Insurance Portability and Accountability Act (HIPAA)	US healthcare providers, payers, clearing houses, and their business associates	Privacy	Protect the security and privacy of personally identifiable health information from unauthorized access, alteration, deletion, or transmission.
Gramm-Leach-Bliley Act (GLBA)	US-based financial institutions	Privacy	Establish administrative, physical, and technical safeguards to protect the security, confidentiality, and integrity of consumer financial information.

(continued)

Table 8-1. (*continued*)

Regulation	Organizations Affected	Focus	Information Security Requirements
North American Electric Reliability Council (NERC)	All entities responsible for planning, operating, and using the bulk electric system in North America	Critical infrastructure protection	Protect IT assets essential to the reliability of the bulk electric system, including monitoring, access control, and change/configuration management.
CA Senate Bill (SB) 1386 and 46 other state regulations	Organizations that store personal data	Privacy	Alert individuals when personal data is lost or stolen.

Taking the right approach to compliance can enable an organization to manage user access as a sustainable ongoing process, rather than a one-time audit event that does little to support a sustainable, secure computing environment.

Sustainable Compliance

To proactively address compliance requirements, many organizations look to Identity Governance to define and manage the overall process. Identity Governance is a cross-organizational enterprise discipline that provides the intelligence and business insights needed to strengthen controls and protect information assets. With Identity Governance, organizations gain a 360-degree control plane that answers the question "who has access to what." This control plane provides the process and tracking transparency needed to reduce potential security and compliance exposures.

Identity Governance also helps organizations improve efficiency by replacing paper-based manual processes with automated tools. Not only can an organization significantly reduce the cost of compliance, but it also helps establish a repeatable process that is more consistent, auditable, and reliable over time. Taking an automated approach helps to build predictability, repeatability, and sustainability into the compliance workflows while improving the end-user experience and overall satisfaction.

Building a Repeatable Process

The following steps describe a base methodology and timeline for implementing Identity Governance. The key to success is defining measurable steps to build that repeatable and sustainable compliance process across all identity tasks and activities. Table 8-2 shows the commonly employed best practice approach to achieving this goal.

Table 8-2. *Best practice steps toward sustainable compliance and Identity Governance*

1 Assess Your Current State	2 Build Governance Model	3 Automate Detective Controls	4 Automate Preventative Controls	5 Perform Closed-Loop Audit on All Changes
Aggregate and correlate identity data	Define policy model	Access certifications	Access request management	Aggregate data
Conduct baseline access certification	Define role model	Policy detection and remediation	Password management	Identity exceptions
	Define risk model		Automated provisioning	Provide proof of compliance

CHAPTER 9

Indicators of Compromise

There are plenty of solutions that can help provide indicators of compromise (IoC). Some will highlight the IP address of an asset, the malware detected, or even unusual patterns in user behavior. All of these can be mapped back to the three pillars of cybersecurity discussed earlier in the book. The goal of IoC is to identify when something is inappropriate in an environment, what evidence supports the anomaly, and potentially the root cause from malware to insider threat. With this in mind, there are four aspects that can create an IoC:

1. The entitlements assigned to an identity which are misused or hijacked

2. The inappropriate assignment of entitlements and their potential abuse

3. Any access and entitlement change made outside of established Identity Governance controls and oversight.

4. Misuse of the Identity Governance system itself to compromise the environment

This translates into two forms of IoC analysis. One that parses the entitlements for an identity, their associated accounts on potentially every resource, and documents their entitlements for reconciliation. The second is based on user behavior. It is an active analysis of an identity and their interaction with resources to determine the risk of their behavior. Essentially this asks the question, was the user acting appropriately for their role? And, was it the right human persona or was their identity compromised and their access rights abused? When end users embrace these concepts from an academic level, they realize very quickly that technology has been created to simplify Identity Governance best practices, but implementation gaps tend to make the results impractical without adhering to some additional best practices as we have previously discussed. These are all in the form of account creation and nomenclature.

© Morey J. Haber, Darran Rolls 2020
M. J. Haber and D. Rolls, *Identity Attack Vectors*, https://doi.org/10.1007/978-1-4842-5165-2_9

As an exercise, let us explore the identity for a fictional, albeit typical user. For this example, we will leverage John Titor again since he has already been established as a threat actor engaged in identity theft.

Within Active Directory (AD), John has a username associated with him. This username allows him to access Windows resources and any other solutions linked via Active Directory Federation Services (ADFS) or via an alternative single sign-on (SSO) solution.

John also has a secondary account in AD that allows him to function as an administrator with elevated rights as a member of the help desk. This means John has two accounts associated with his identity, both of which must be mapped back to his identity in order to track user activity and entitlement usage.

If we add his macOS, Unix, Linux, and other infrastructure access to this picture, we can increase the number of accounts and entitlements associated with John into hundreds. Tracking an IoC to the correct identity then becomes an art rather than an academic exercise – especially if security best practices are followed to obfuscate the username to something cryptic vs. user identifiable. For example, John's username may be "jtitor" and easily identifiable, but some organizations, based on regulatory compliance or security best practices, may choose another schema that makes the association very difficult without an external reference database. That is something the account and entitlement mapping inside the Identity Governance solution can help reconcile.

To that end, and for our example, John's obfuscated username could be "NY2036," and his administrator account could look completely different. I think this helps explain the complexity of mapping any discovered entitlements or user behavior to the proper identity. Identity Governance tools can help discover NY2036, but it would have to be manually linked back to John before it could be used by forensics tools when discovering IoCs.

As a best practice, to simplify the process of mapping the proper identity to accounts and making it easy to discover IoCs, organizations should attempt to

- Maintain a full map of accounts back to users using an Identity Governance solution

- Minimize the number of service accounts associated with an identity

- Use a directory bridge to authenticate with one centralized authoritative source, like AD

- Avoid sharing credentials (especially administrator or root) with multiple identities

A second implementation gap is bidirectional in nature. We may understand what an identity is supposed to do (entitlements) and what it actually did (session monitoring), but deciding on whether or not the overlap was appropriate is definitely an art.

For example, if John is a senior database administrator (DBA), he should be allowed to run virtually any command on a database resource for maintenance, upgrades, and backups and to correct problems. In this example, John may have a junior DBA, Larry. As a subordinate to John, Larry should not have the same privileges. If John and Larry are two different identities that share the same account, there may be no way to determine who (without significant forensic investigation) actually ran the commands, whether or not they were correct, and, most importantly, were they appropriate.

John and Larry should not have the same entitlements, but if they share the same accounts, they do. This leads to some additional best practices that organizations should adhere to:

- Every identity should have unique accounts associated with it – accounts should not be shared whenever and wherever possible.

- An identity's entitlements should also map to real user behavior in the privileged access management system.

- User behavior should be mapped back to entitlements (bidirectional) to determine if behavior is appropriate.

Using identities as an indicator of compromise can be a complex undertaking. It may sound simple on paper, but account implementations within most organizations significantly complicate the process and can hinder any threat hunting initiatives. A security team must be able to use their Identity Governance solution to map all accounts to an identity and, in doing so, create a clear path to determine inappropriate behavior.

CHAPTER 10

Identity Attack Vectors

An identity attack vector can effect the person owning the identity or any part of the connected chain down to the applications, accounts, passwords and privileges they execute. If it could not, there would be no purpose for this book! As an attack surface, we need to think beyond traditional ports, protocols, and services found in traditional IT security defense thinking. Identity attack vectors have a risk surface that is not only electronic, but also physical, and can be compromised using old-school paper communications, such as a letter from the postal service or social engineering using the plain old telephone system.

However, the point of an identity attack is fairly straightforward. A threat actor wants to find a method to compromise an identity and impersonate it for their own malicious intent. All they need to do is get access to one of your accounts to get started. If it is a privileged account, it is nearly "game over" from the start. The goal of the threat actor is to own you at the highest level possible and impersonate you as far down the account chain as possible. To be clear, they want to be an electronic impostor. The threat actor's goal is to disrupt the one-to-one relationship of a person to their identity and then compromise the integrity of the identity-to-account relationship. So, the risk surface encompasses all the methods to disrupt these relationships. This threat model applies to both physical and electronic identities.

Once a threat actor can successfully impersonate you, they can authenticate with your accounts – assuming your authorization has not been restricted – and own your identity. The attacker then assumes the ability to perform the tasks you are privileged to perform, and using other attack vectors, potentially elevates their privileges to administrator or root. This is why maintaining a complete map of identity and account relationships, and understanding how they can be used for IoCs, is so important.

© Morey J. Haber, Darran Rolls 2020
M. J. Haber and D. Rolls, *Identity Attack Vectors*, https://doi.org/10.1007/978-1-4842-5165-2_10

Methods

What methods does a threat actor leverage to steal your identity? In an electronic world, they go after your accounts. They steal the associated credentials via some vulnerability and exploit related assets or leverage privileged attack vectors against available accounts.

In a physical world, criminals attempt social engineering, mail fraud, stealing identification, or even tricking you into committing to verbal or written actions. While physical identity theft can result in fraudulent loans, credit cards opened under your name, or even purchases made on your behalf, physical identity theft typically translates into an electronic form at some juncture in the attack chain. Only physical impersonations of claiming to be someone, such as by wearing their uniform and name badge, stay manifest purely in the physical world. The damage a threat actor can perform can be severe if they also have stolen your electronic identity as well. Edward Snowden demonstrated the ramifications of this electronic identity attack, which he perpetrated even while he was a trusted insider. He did not need to perform any physical impersonations to steal all the information he did. He did, however, steal the credential from his colleagues.

To that end, the following are methods a threat actor will use to exploit an identity risk surface:

- **Electronic**
  - **Vulnerabilities and Exploits** – Software flaws that can lead to exploitation and ownership of an account
  - **Misconfigurations** – Poor configuration hygiene that can allow an attacker to hijack or create accounts
  - **Privileged Attacks** – Credential and password attacks based on poor account hygiene that give a threat actor unintentional access
  - **Social Engineering** – Broad electronic misuse to target a person to obtain sensitive information

- **Physical**

    - **Imposter** – A physical representation of another person for the sake of inappropriate access

    - **Documentation** – False physical paperwork designed to invoke a state of compromise and mislead the target to provide information or access

    - **Audible** – Verbal command or responsive social engineering typically done over the phone or via an always-listening microphone to capture sensitive information or grant unintended privileges

    - **Biometric** – The theft and malicious implementation of biometric data to gain access or compromise additional datasets

These are all basic classifications but nonetheless form the basis for every breach we experience today. All of these can be linked back to an identity and used as an attack vector.

Tactics

Today, the favored tactic used by threat actors for bulk compromise of accounts is the Dark Web. This is where illicitly obtained information (account names, passwords, and configuration information) is traded between criminals in the form of raw data, or even as a service to target the new exfiltration of more data. This information may have details regarding a user's identity (like address and phone number), but luckily, today we rarely see information linking an identity to multiple accounts in order to build a complete identity profile. If this mapping is done, fields like email addresses could provide the correlation rules needed (as we have already discussed), and basic identity attributes could provide the linkage needed for a threat actor to own your identity at home, or at work.

While individual attacks may be opportunistic or targeted, large-scale attacks are typically based on some form of identified financial gain and, as such, will target accounts that have already been compromised. This could be an attempt to steal additional data or start the process of a ransomware infection. Tactics for identity theft can be performed by

- The art of hacking one person at a time by any means available to the threat actor including targeted attacks with detailed information about the user

- Bulk premeditated attacks using techniques like credential stuffing or brute force attacks to compromise vulnerable accounts

- Targeting vendors and the supply chain or contractors and seasonal workers or simply "fuzzing" the externally available APIs – basically attacking anything that is available and accessible outside of the organization and vulnerable to an attack due to insecure credential practices and dormant accounts.

All of these apply to both insider threats and external attacks. With these in mind, the most common methods threat actors use to compromise an account and escalate to an identity are the following:

- **Interception** – Passwords are captured as they are transmitted electronically through email, the network, and even SMS texts. This includes SMS cloning, SIM-jacking or other forms of hijacking and man-in-the-middle attacks.

- **Brute Force** – Automated guessing of passwords using dictionaries or other related password libraries (often called Rainbow Tables) that target password reuse.

- **Searching** – The manual or electronic searching of passwords stored in insecure files, scripts, or other inappropriate electronic medium. This also falls under the category of sensitive, unstructured data abuses.

- **Manual Guessing** – Based on social engineering and knowledge of the identity, a threat actor will try to manually guess the password for an account.

- **Social Engineering** – Threat actors use human trust and social interaction to trick an identity into revealing credentials or other sensitive information.

- **Stealing Passwords** – The theft of passwords that are insecurely stored on paper or other non-electronic media. This could be as simple as posting a secure Wi-Fi password on the whiteboard of a conference room or the now mythical post-it note under the keyboard.

- **Shoulder Surfing** – Physically observing someone typing in their password by looking over their shoulder. This could also be done electronically when a camera either in the user's device or close to a desk has been compromised.

- **Key Logging** – Malware used to capture sensitive keystrokes, including passwords, as they are being entered and then transmitted to or retrieved by the threat actor for later reuse.

Once passwords have been stolen, they are used by the threat actor directly or placed on the Dark Web for sale to the highest bidder. In reality, the Dark Web is nothing more than a collection of criminally inclined web sites that use service models to transact the purchase of passwords, tools, and data to leverage the stolen information. Regardless, the tactics are the same once the data is exposed; leverage it to steal more account and data and escalate "ownership" to the identity level.

In addition, threat actors from nation states and organized criminal entities don't rely entirely on the Dark Web for their mission intel. They often operate as the sources of Dark Web data and can be actively engaged in attacking organizations to obtain illegal information in the first place. These criminal entities may build a long-term persistent presence to realize their goals while building extensive profiles of identities and access in order to fuel future attacks. These organizations are typically well-funded, and their motives for identity theft go far beyond the quick monetization of the stolen information. Again, the discovery and reconciliation processes advocated by an Identity Governance program form a very effective method for determining deviations in established business rules that could be used as IoCs for these types of persistent threats.

Implications

The implications of identity theft can be profound, disheartening, and even gruesome. The elderly (often targets of consumer identity theft) can have all of their financial savings depleted. For a business, it could mean the large-scale theft of intellectual property or, more profoundly, even an event that causes major financial disruption to normal operations. These breaches have been in the news for years and are not expected to subside anytime soon. Even the deceased can have their identities or accounts compromised in ways that make it difficult for their heirs to reconcile their estates. This brings into question how every business deals with a "leaver" situation. These event are not always planned or palatable and can be as unplanned as a sudden employee death or mass catastrophic event like 9/11. Organizations find it difficult to manage these situations without a comprehensive approach to governance. If accounts and users are not managed after an unexpected event, the ramifications can be long-lasting for the health of the business and everyone concerned.

To illustrate how depraved a threat actor may act to achieve their goals, consider the following: A recent, far-reaching data breach in South Africa involved all the typical traits of a government or credit reporting service compromise. Within the data sets stolen was an interesting user attribute field not commonly seen in other breaches – "deceased status." This personally identifiable information contained data on whether the identity associated with the account was alive or dead. While it did not reveal the date of their death, it did open a very morbid question, "Can you better attack the dead rather than the living? The simple and grave answer is "yes."

Taking this to another morbid level of extreme, consider an individual who is recently deceased:

- Their bank accounts have not been closed or frozen nor their employer's ability for direct deposit.

- Social media sites may allow active postings, and messages including ones used for business activities.

- They probably still receive email at work and home.

- Their cell phones and landlines may still work including voice mail.

- They may not have loved ones immediately available to manage their estates.

All of the preceding scenarios make their estate a prime target for identity theft. The cybercriminals could siphon off, or even liquidate, the deceased's assets since, potentially, no one is monitoring their assets, services, and resources. Considering the interconnected financial world we live in, hacking the dead may seem like a morbid topic, but evidence suggest that these types of targeted attacks are increasing and most organizations appear not to be protecting an identity well in these scenarios. The implications are the same for other similar change triggers like extended illness, maternity leave, and sabbaticals. All of these long-term status changes must be a part of your governance model for controls and oversight to help prevent unmonitored identity attack vectors.

Privileges

Identity attack vectors have two real-world implications, regardless of the methods and tactics employed. These attacks could affect you regardless of whether you are a consumer or operating in a business context. In all cases, the goal of the attacker is to gain access to your privileges and entitlements. Let's start with a worst case and assume your identity has been compromised. This means a threat actor(s) has access to your account(s). The type of account compromised, privileged, standard user, or shared/guest, tells us how much damage they can actually do to your identity without additional attack vectors. In addition, how many accounts are compromised, and their financial or legal importance also implies how much cost could be involved to undo the damage. This is true for a business or consumer account.

The privileges and entitlements your identity has are extremely relevant to a threat actor. For example, if you are a doctor, and your identity is stolen, through the exploitation of your account, the adversary may have access to patient records. The privileges in this case only matter as much as the entitlements granted to you and the resources available to that account. As the doctor, you are not the administrator for the application itself, but typically would have privileges to retrieve sensitive information for all of your patients. This makes your identity and the accounts and entitlements you have a more valuable target and therefore puts you at a high risk. In this scenario, the only higher risk would be presented by the system administrator for the application or someone with access to its supporting infrastructure. If either of their "classic" privileged identities is compromised, not only is it possible that the application is at risk but all the data and all the users of that resource will be at risk as well. Knowing who these account owners are and monitoring their access is key in mitigating identity attack vectors.

This scenario exemplifies why you must understand privileged entitlement and helps underscore that users should always be given the least amount of privileges possible. This can be accomplished using clearly defined privilege management processes and leveraging Identity Governance and PAM solutions.

Regardless of its electronic demark (including remote access), accounts should always have at least three different types of account privileges. Remember, an identity can have multiple accounts, and each one should have the lowest form of privileges. While each of these can have granularity within them, a privileged account is typically the highest level of rights, while "None" contains no rights whatsoever and is actually lower than Guest access. This is the first implication of identity attack vectors. A threat actor directly gaining privileged access to an account assigned administrative privileges and owned by an important identity is the worst-case scenario for any organization. The second implication is the converse. A threat actor directly gaining privileged access to the high-level administrative privileges for "powerful" identity can be the worst-case scenario for any organization. The latter can be managed by Endpoint Detection and Response (EDR) solutions, while the former typically cannot since it is typically modeled as authorized privileged activity. User behavioral analytics has a more difficult time interpreting malicious activity when valid credentials are being used and the account itself is already considered privileged.

In the world of Identity and Access Management (IAM), all accounts, and their associated credentials, can be placed under management regardless of the privileges. This helps mitigate the threats from both scenarios. In the world of Privileged Access Management (PAM), typically only accounts with administrative, root, or super user privileges are placed under management. The latter, as we have concluded, is what threat actors seek. However, if they can gain access to even a lower-level attack, privileged attack vectors or asset attack vectors can be leveraged to elevate threat actor's rights. This is how an incident can turn into a full-fledged breach. In Figure 10-1, this is illustrated as the privileged attack chain.

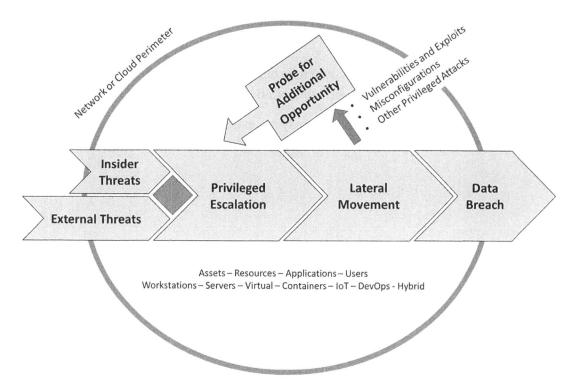

Figure 10-1. *Privileged attack chain*

With this in mind, here are the definitions for each user account type that can be under IAM management:

- **Privileged User** – A privileged user is typically the administrator or root for a resource.

- **Super User** – A super user (or superuser) has elevated privileges in various graduations above a standard user, but does not have full administrative capabilities.

- **Standard User** – A standard user is void of all elevated privileges except for normal runtime of a resource.

- **Guest** – A guest is the lowest form of access and is typically below a standard user. Interaction with a guest account only provides basic services.

- **Anonymous** – Control access to specific resources only using an account with a null password or keys not exposed to the end user.

- **Disabled** – A disabled account may have any level of privileges, but is explicitly denied access and interaction with assigned resources.

- **None** – No privileges at all and may not even be defined as an identity or account.

CHAPTER 11

Identity Management Controls in the Cyber Kill Chain

Managing and appropriately governing identities using an Identity Governance solution can make a big difference to the security posture of an organization. To best understand how, we must first learn from our collective past mistakes and omissions. Looking back over recent data breach reports and examining the forensic and post-incident analysis, we notice two things relative to the discussion on identity management controls. The first is that threat sophistication is increasing at a furious rate. The adversary is persistent and well funded and knows where best to attack and pursue persistence. The second is that these forensic reports clearly show that identity management mistakes and weaknesses are the common faults in many breaches. These identity management mistakes and process weaknesses are things like poor account controls; weak passwords; orphan, dormant, and rogue accounts; weak inventory of entitlements; and the over-assignment of user privileges. These mistakes and management missteps tend to be spread across the Cyber Kill Chain.

The Cyber Kill Chain

The Cyber Kill Chain was introduced by Lockheed Martin in the late 1990s and documents the anatomy of a typical cyber breach by plotting the path of attack from start to finish. In many ways, it has become a reference model for cyber defense thinking for more than 20 years.

© Morey J. Haber, Darran Rolls 2020
M. J. Haber and D. Rolls, *Identity Attack Vectors*, https://doi.org/10.1007/978-1-4842-5165-2_11

There are many derivatives of the Cyber Kill Chain approach. We introduced one earlier in this book with the privileged attack chain. We now want to take this concept further and use a view of the formal attack phases to help us better understand where identity attack vectors are exposed and best mitigated.

Figure 11-1 shows this further adaptation of the formal Cyber Kill Chain model that we will use to highlight where weakness in the IAM system (and its controls) are often at fault. This goes beyond the formal list of identity attack vectors introduced in Chapter 4 and examines the flaws in the underlying systems and infrastructure that get exploited.

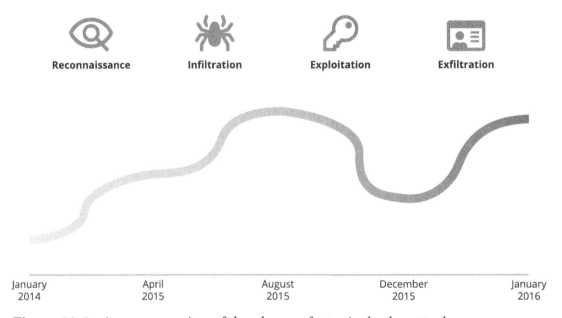

Figure 11-1. *A summary view of the phases of a typical cyberattack*

In the following text, we will use this fictional attack timeline to plot the details and actions of a real-world cyberattack. The details are, in fact, derived from several recent actual breach reports with all identifying information suitably removed. We will first draw out on this timeline how things went wrong. We then come back around and review the same timeline with an emphasis on how and where IAM could have helped prevent and detect the breach. This is set against an event timeline that started in 2016. Analysis of that event and others just like it shows that an average attack can last between 200 and 300 days. Here we see an extended period spanning nearly two years from April 2015 through January 2016.

Reconnaissance

For this breach, things start as they often do with active reconnaissance. The elements of this attack phase are summarized in Figure 11-2. The first phase of the Cyber Kill Chain is all about the adversary gaining knowledge on the target and how best to attack it. As a starting tactic, the attacker will often begin scanning all the externally facing web and network resources the target enterprise has available.

This phase is also when social engineering begins. Anyone and everyone connected with the company – employees, customers, vendors, partners, and so on – will be researched, and those with potential access into the enterprise will be sent blanket phishing emails. Executives and other high-value targets will usually be subject to these spear-phishing campaigns.

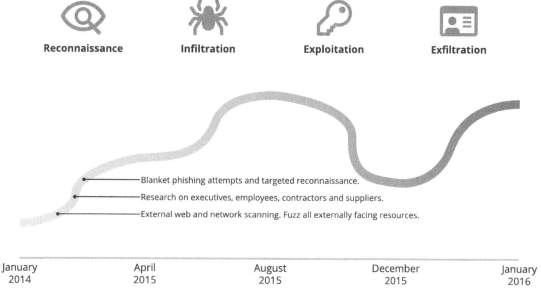

Figure 11-2. Reconnaissance Phase IAM weaknesses

Infiltration

The next phase of our Kill Chain is infiltration; this is summarized in Figure 11-3. With ever-increasing numbers of people accessing our systems and data, eventually someone always makes a mistake. Often that mistake is simply clicking the wrong link in the wrong email. Spear-phishing has become so sophisticated and so widespread that in our scenario, an executive clicked a link that downloaded a basic "drive-by" malware exploit onto their computer. With that exploit successfully executed, the local admin account could be compromised, and the bad guys have access to a wide range of enterprise network resources. With a local admin access, the attacker could move laterally with virtually no limits to attack the organization's servers, install required attack tooling, and begin scanning the network for further weaknesses.

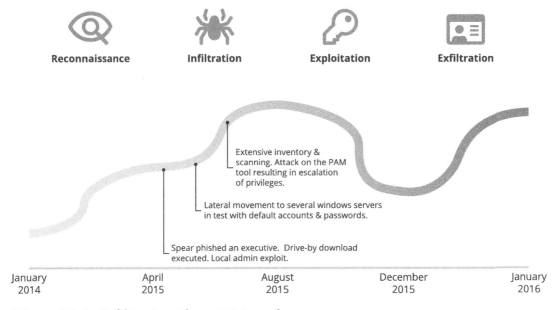

Figure 11-3. *Infiltration Phase IAM weaknesses*

Exploitation

During this phase of the attack, the attackers have found their way into several resources and are looking for the best ways to gain higher levels of privilege and access to the most valuable data resources. This phase of the attack is highlighted in Figure 11-4. We usually see brute force password attacks on administrative accounts as the most common identity attack vector here. The goal is to compromise more accounts and move laterally. We often see attacks on business processes such as manual access requests and end-user self-service capabilities. When a system of requesting and gaining access is executed over email, messages are easily spoofed, and incorrect access is often granted.

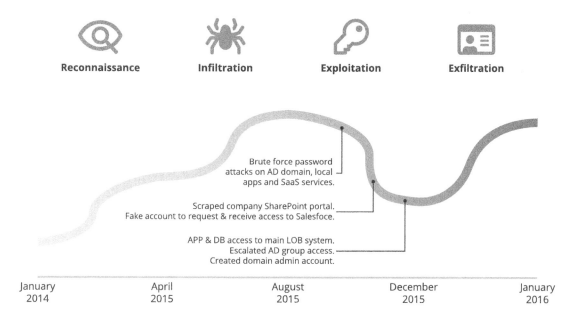

Figure 11-4. Exploitation Phase IAM weaknesses

Exfiltration

Once a good set of target systems are owned, the last phase of the Kill Chain is the exfiltration of data. This is shown in Figure 11-5. This usually involves downloading password databases for internal systems, the collection of customer data, and the theft of intellectual property. We also see archiving and removal of large number of files from internal and cloud file storage systems at this time. And lastly, in more recent attacks, we see the use of ransomware to hold the organization hostage after the adversary has "left the building."

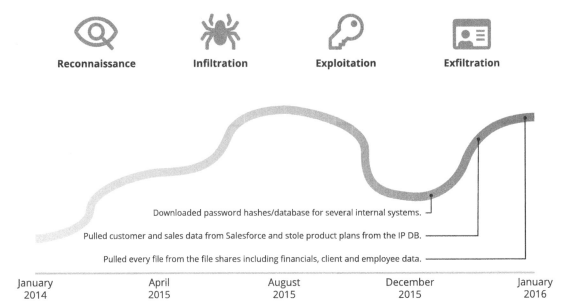

Figure 11-5. *Exploitation Phase IAM weaknesses*

Fixing IAM Gaps and Overlaying Governance Controls

With modern identity management software at hand, we can prevent many of the mistakes seen across the typical Cyber Kill Chain. Using IAM best practices, we can overlay governance controls to protect known weaknesses and set out additional detection capabilities that improve situational awareness.

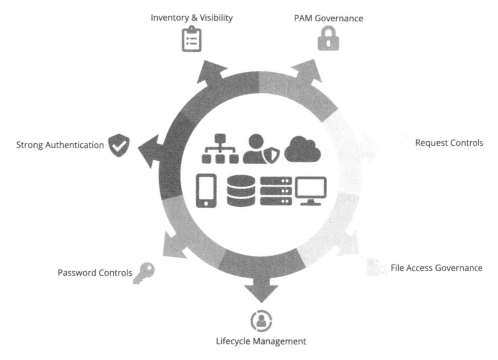

Figure 11-6. *Enhanced IAM protection and detection capabilities*

In Figure 11-6, we show the array of enhanced IAM protection and detection capabilities available on the market today. These capabilities can be applied across the Cyber Kill Chain. We will now look at each of these capabilities in turn and show how they should be used to create a different outcome:

- **Weak Inventory and Cataloging** – Default accounts and passwords used during lateral movement can be aggregated, certified, and automatically remediated. Orphan account management can detect the creation of new admin accounts used by attackers. An automated recertification can also be used to highlight escalation of privileges that tends to happen over an extended period.

- **Strong Authentication** – Strong multifactor authentication and context aware login can prevent and detect lots of issues in the flow of the kill chain. With strong controls over sign-on, internal security teams can identify administrative access that happens at unusual times and from unusual locations. This is true for managing access to the IAM tools themselves. For example, strong authentication should always be used when logging into an Identity Governance system.

123

- **Password Controls** – Good password management controls play a significant part in preventing and slowing down the progress of an attack. Strong password policies make cracking and brute-force password attacks computationally time-consuming and costly for the attacker. Identity Governance lifecycle triggers can also be used to alert the security team that account passwords were changing outside of policy controls.

- **Lifecycle Management** – Account Lifecycle Management sets out an operational baseline for both prevention and detection of compromise. Implementing strong JML state transition controls can help detect out-of-policy changes to the overall assigned entitlement model. Embedded data triggers can easily be used to alert admins and security staff when entitlements are changing. And detective controls and policy checks can catch the escalation of privileges that inevitably happened during a successful attack.

- **PAM Governance** – The inventory and modeling of any deployed Privilege Account Management (PAM) infrastructure proves essential additional controls and governance. Applying the full suite of IGA best practices to the entitlements managed by the PAM tier is also essential to prevent and detect an attack. We must deliver visibility and certification for access to PAM systems as they are a focus point for attacks. Administrator and root accounts are the keys to the kingdom and the target goal of a threat actor when trying to infiltrate an environment. Inventorying and modeling PAM system assignment and usage, creation, and entitlements is key in preventing identity-based attack vectors.

- **Request Controls** – Approvals and audit for all new access changes stop the adversary from circumnavigating manual request and fulfillment systems. Preventive policy evaluation helps ensure that only the right people have access and allowing IT security staff to focus on the areas of highest risk.

- **File Access Governance** – Effective access modeling, data classification, and file access alerts are key controls available throughout the Cyber Kill Chain. During the ever-shortening exfiltration phase, file access governance techniques are an essential means of detecting the kinds of file access events typical to this phase.

CHAPTER 12

Identity Management Program Planning

Over the years, we've seen what makes organizations successful and, sometimes more interestingly, not so successful, when dealing with large-scale Identity Governance projects. We often get asked to leverage these experiences to shape customers' identity management strategy and provide a blueprint for success. This chapter outlines some of our observations and recommendations to get you thinking about the basic necessities that form the foundation of an effective identity management strategy.

Program vs. Project

Before we begin, let's clear up some important terminology – the difference between a *program* and a *project*. People incorrectly use these terms interchangeably, and in the context of the following guidance, it is important to understand the difference. While *programs* and *projects* both have specific directives, and they are both a key to success, there is a big difference in how they function relative to a complex transformational process like Identity Governance.

A *project* is an individual or collaborative effort that is carefully planned and executed, to fulfill a particular goal, for instance, an implementation which focuses on certain deliverables. A *program* is a set of related activities, events, or maybe projects with a particular long-term goal. It is therefore important that we do not confuse singular project delivery with strategic, long-term program planning.

When considering identity management in general, too many people focus on the project and not the program. Completing an identity-related project doesn't make you successful with an identity management program. An identity management program must be established and nurtured over time, as it is designed to continually deliver and evolve with the business, following a clear roadmap for program success.

© Morey J. Haber, Darran Rolls 2020
M. J. Haber and D. Rolls, *Identity Attack Vectors*, https://doi.org/10.1007/978-1-4842-5165-2_12

Based on this definition, Identity Management *projects* should be used to deliver functionality phases, as part of a long-term Identity Management *program*.

Establishing an Identity Governance Program

An Identity Governance program definition is your foundation for success. But how is this program typically structured? What are the key components to help you meet your operational efficiency, security, and governance goals? A good starting point is to understand the roles and responsibilities for the teams that need to be engaged and to list out the key components of a successful program approach.

Key Roles and Responsibilities

There are several key roles and responsibilities required to create a good foundation for an Identity Governance program. It's critical to have an executive sponsor, a steering committee, and one or more program managers. These roles and responsibilities are explained in the following.

The **executive sponsor** is the figurehead, champion, and owner of the program. It is important that this person has "organizational influence." A good executive sponsor likely has board-level exposure and is responsible for ensuring the program stays relevant and visible to the business as a whole. This involves securing an adequate and consistent source of funding and reporting on the impact the program is having back to the business as a whole.

The **steering committee** is a set of aligned stakeholders who meet on a regular basis to track, monitor, and evaluate program progress and success. Committee members are usually people from cross-functional departments who have organizations control and prioritization influence and can therefore help address issues relative to the Identity Governance program charter should they arise. The steering committee helps the program remain relevant to the wider business as a whole.

Every organization is different; therefore, the composition of its steering committee usually varies accordingly. *Adequate representation of key stakeholders is critically important to the success of an Identity Governance program.* A typical steering committee will consist of representatives from Human Resources (HR), Information Security (IS), Information Technology (IT), and Compliance/Audit and from the "line of business" – the people who drive the specifics of the business you are in. Without a steering committee, programs tend to have a niche view of an organization's needs, and the Identity Governance program can easily become an isolated project rather than a program driving improvements in operational efficiency, security, and compliance.

A **program manager** helps coordinate and run the program, whether that means managing and coordinating several projects at once or managing the wider influence of the governance program as a whole. Having a clearly defined program manager or managers is essential to meeting Identity Governance deployment success.

Key Program Components

Every program has a set of key components that help define how it executes. It is important to establish these early in the process and continually evaluate their efficacy and relevance as the program matures over time.

Most successful programs typically start by defining a clear and concise **program charter**. This is defined by the steering committee and ratified in the form of a mission statement, business case, and agreed-upon purpose for the program. A charter captures the spirit of the program and may help defend its existence. An Identity Governance program can never be designed in a vacuum or defined by a single person's perspective. Your program charter should be clearly approved and "signed-off" before moving onto the next component. It should also be revisited regularly, to make sure that it stays relevant to the business over time.

After the program charter is approved, **program funding** is necessary to deliver on that charter. This can come in a variety of forms, from a single cost-center budget to a managed cross-departmental resource pool and every possible form in between. Programs deliver long-term vision and value to the organization, so a consistent and reliable source of funding is essential to enable it to continue to deliver on that vision over time.

A high-level **program roadmap** should be defined to outline the long-term plan and business case timeline. This is essential for program definition and funding. An Identity Governance program should evangelize the long-term plan but march toward short-term goals and project milestones that can be met along a defined roadmap. Delivering results in smaller iterations helps return value to the business faster and allows for a flexible long-term plan with well-scoped short-term deliverables that show progress and business benefits.

Well-managed programs will also have a **program log** to capture decisions made, deliverables met, issues raised and addressed, risks encountered, and a record of the overall progress toward the programs' goals and roadmap. This historical record can be an essential artifact in helping to document and justify program efficacy. A detailed program log is often necessary to demonstrate program accountability and ensure ongoing funding and support.

It may seem obvious or trivial, but we also strongly recommend defining and maintaining a baseline **program terminology** document to help make requirements and meanings clear to everyone involved. This also helps get participants engaged and speaking the same language. Try to use established industry terms where possible and involve any contractors, consultants, and third parties that will be working on a project or engaged in the program as a whole.

Program Roadmap Questions

Everyone would like a predefined, vendor-prescribed program roadmap for Identity Governance. In reality, each organization's roadmap will be very specific to its business drivers, its industry vertical, and the history and challenges of its specific needs. That said, there are several predefined questions that you should ask to help guide your program roadmap prioritization process.

We recommend posing the following questions to a cross-functional group and providing the program steering committee with full visibility into the answers. This helps achieve a cohesive and representative starting state that sets the scope and boundaries of your Identity Governance program charter.

What is most important to your organization?

Your answer to this question will vary over time. What is important to your organization today may not be important to you tomorrow, next quarter, or next year. Organizations are continually changing and going through expansion, contraction, mergers, acquisitions, reorganizations, and divestitures. These changes will directly impact your Identity Governance program prioritization and influence your deployment roadmap. It is therefore essential that you regularly reask these questions at defined intervals to see if the pulse of your organization has changed.

Where is the biggest impact or pain point?

At first glance, asking this question may seem redundant. But having the biggest impact, or solving the biggest problem, may not be the ultimate driver for selecting program bounds. Posing this question is more about identifying areas where distractions and road blocks will come from. Of course, it can just as easily point directly to the most immediate driver and program funding source.

Are there any easy-to-achieve goals or quick wins?

Documenting the perceived easy-to-achieve goals or quick wins is again an obvious question to ask. Identifying what's relatively easy and ready to implement without additional research, discovery, analysis, or implementation effort is important. However, what's easy to deliver may not align with the impact or importance of the program to the supporting organization. That said, identifying and delivering quick wins in a noncritical area can help build confidence in the governance program as a whole and so should be considered regardless of where it fits in the roadmap.

Are there any areas which are risky or more susceptible to change?

Answering this question is about understanding where the potential risks to your program roadmap lie and minimizing the risk of rework, re-implementation, or redesign. If an area of your organization is currently undergoing significant change, it might be best to invest in delivering functionality elsewhere first and revisit that area in a later phase.

The Seven-Step Program Roadmap Model

After gaining an understanding of your organizational priorities, we recommend you take an iterative approach to implementing your program strategy. We've observed that customers with smaller, tightly scoped deliverables are generally more successful than those who try to deliver too much at once. We strongly recommend you think in terms of delivering several smaller projects rather than "big bangs." This helps establish credibility and puts your overall program on a positive footing early in its lifecycle.

The following seven-step phased model is offered as a starting point and general guideline for your Identity Governance program. For each project phase, we offer a description of its purpose and provide both a **project goal** and a **program objective** to help you understand its purpose and justification. Please note that this model is just a guideline and a generic set of recommendations. Your project can and very likely will approach things differently based on your needs. Many customers have been successful following a totally different set of project steps, in a completely different order. Many have focused on a subset of these recommendations – all for good business reasons and most with a successful outcome. Your Identity Governance program requirements ultimately must drive your project phase decisions. With that caveat duly noted, please also understand that these are high-level deliverable phases that can and often do get broken down into smaller pieces as needed.

One quick spoiler alert: Phase 7, password management, can and often does fit anywhere in the process between phases 2 and 6; we cover exactly why that is the case in the description that follows.

1. Identity Foundation

- ***Project Goal*** *– Connect to authoritative sources, build an identity model, and analyze data.*

- ***Program Objective*** *– Build a foundational model of people in the organization, setting the stage for future work.*

The first phase of establishing an Identity Governance program is to build a foundational model of the people in your organization. This involves connecting to any authoritative sources and understanding the identity data. Identity data covers the employees, contractors, contingent workers, or third parties under consideration. Having Human Resources (HR) as a stakeholder on the steering committee early on helps shape this effort.

During this phase, data about the identities starts to take shape. The goal is to analyze the data looking for errors, inconsistencies, and missing information. As part of this phase, you will want to assess what to do with any anomalies found; This may involve addressing them directly at the source-feed and re-aggregating, or using the data transform and mapping capabilities of the governance tool. At a program level, deciding how you will handle good and bad data in your organization can set the precedence for future Identity Governance program work.

2. Source Onboarding/Access Review

- ***Project Goal*** *– Connect to sources, and review and understand access.*

- ***Program Objective*** *– Understand access models, and clean/remove unnecessary access for future phases.*

The second phase of establishing an Identity Governance program is to onboard application sources for user account and access information. This is about making sure that accounts relate back to the identity model previously established.

The application sources you connect to will vary based on your program scope and your application risk landscape. As already discussed, we believe in smaller iterative phases to deliver a successful project, so we do not recommend immediately connecting to *every source* or business application in your company's portfolio. Instead, prioritize key, high-value, or easily implemented sources first. In an initial phase, customers commonly connect to sources such as Active Directory (or generic LDAP directories), SSO solutions, and SOX-relevant applications.

Resist the temptation to try and automate *all sources* with direct connections. While this may be technically feasible, it might not be worth the implementation investment to manage users and access in a system involving a small percentage of users or access or minimal change. As a general rule of thumb, direct connectors typically don't make sense in an early phase if they represent less than 10% of your overall identity population. The exception here being applications with high levels of user churn or mission-critical risk factors identified in the program justification. In general terms, there tends to be a diminishing return on investment connecting to sources with low numbers of user accounts.

After sources are onboarded, user accounts and access rights are aggregated into the base Identity Governance platform and correlated back to the core identity model. We then recommend configuring an access review as the next step. This initial review is focused on validation, visibility, and business user engagement rather than mandated compliance. *This is a key point: Access reviews are not just a compliance control. They are also a means of data validation and a way to step the business users through a process of review and responsibility – a process that is essential to achieving increased efficiency, enhanced security, and sustainable compliance.*

Access reviews are sent out on a recurring basis, so the business begins to become familiar with the accesses that people have, and certifiers learn to make sense of what access is needed and what is not. The access review process is an effective catalyst, as it forces updates to access descriptions, or even exploration of what access might mean. With every access review cycle, access descriptions become more meaningful, and certifiers learn more about what access really means. Starting this process early is key to future success of a governance-based approach to identity.

Experience shows that revocation (i.e., access removal) rates spike significantly during the first several cycles of access review. In some cases, we have seen as high as 30% of the current access being removed during this phase! These rates do quickly normalize and level-off, resulting in a fairly consistent approval ratio on certification campaigns in the 2-8% range (excluding known leavers and terminations). When this reduction in revocation rate happens, you'll know that your access reviews have effectively cleaned up old, unnecessary, or unwarranted access; clearing out the cobwebs and setting the stage for future governance phases is very important early in the process.

We recommend starting the access review cycle early in the governance program roadmap. As stated, this is an iterative process that will likely need to continue in parallel as other phases and functionality are delivered by the program. Waiting too long to implement access reviews may also overcomplicate implementation of other capabilities such as role-based access control.

3. Birthright Provisioning

- ***Project Goal*** – *Automate basic joiner and leaver processes.*

- ***Program Objective*** – *Reduce the provisioning burden through automation, allowing focus on further expansion.*

The next phase of work focuses around basic provisioning through Joiner and Leaver processes in your organization. The Joiner process typically entails creation of key, standard-issue accounts (and access) for most identities in the organization. The scope is typically focused around creation of directory, SSO, and domain accounts and enabling basic communications like email, where applicable. The Leaver process typically entails the disabling of all accounts, so that if a person leaves the company, their access to key systems is physically removed or logically suspended.

Automating provisioning is usually highly impactful, as it involves basic security control over who is coming and going in your organization. Provisioning itself is very data dependent, as it involves sending identity data to various systems for account creation. The more well-tested your identity foundation is, and the more steps you've taken to analyze and correct data anomalies, the easier this phase will be.

From an Identity Governance program standpoint, it is best to exercise caution around the scope of this phase. It is very tempting to solve every single provisioning use case through a technical or automated means. This can easily balloon the scope and effort needed to deliver this phase. Once again, it's good to start small and build up over time. Additional provisioning use cases and fine-tuning can be easily added to subsequent phases and project deliverables.

4. Access Request

- **Project Goal** – *Provide interface for requesting access.*

- **Program Objective** – *Reduce the burden through automating ad hoc access requests.*

This phase of work allows end users to request access to various new services and send them through a defined approval processes. Since basic provisioning has already been done through the previous birthright provisioning phase, this extends access into the business with a small amount of additional effort and program cost. This phase involves figuring out which units of access should be requestable. You need to define who should approve new access requests and know how best to describe each of the "requestable units" you are making available. If you followed the six-step process defined here and you have run an initial access review cycle in an earlier phase, the effort you put into understanding access, recording descriptions, and defining ownership will pay big dividends here.

This phase also allows the wider business user community to become familiar with a single way to request access and perform approval processes. This helps control the access process and alleviates ad hoc access requests through the help desk or directly to administrators. Access provisioning can then be sent either via direct connectors to the sources you've onboarded or via established manual execution paths.

This is also a good phase to expand source connectivity and optionally integrate with alternate ticketing solutions such as ServiceNow's Service Desk. While we recommend using the Identity Governance access request interface for all logical access processes, user requests can also be initiated from other supported systems such as ServiceNow's Service Catalog as discussed in another chapter.

5. Role-Based Access Control

- **Project Goal** – *Deliver a role-based access control model for provisioning and deprovisioning.*

- **Program Objective** – *Leverage existing access request and access model knowledge to build out fine-grained permission models.*

During this phase, an initial role-based access control model is built to automatically assign access to identities in your organization, triggering provisioning to new or existing accounts. Whenever identities move within your organization, or leave the organization, access can also be removed using the role-based assignment model. This phase is really about mapping identities and access assignments that are meaningful and relevant to your organization.

As previously discussed, there is no single or universally correct way to build roles for your organization. Designing a role-based access control model involved deciding how your organization wants to arrange and assign its specific accesses. There are a number of factors which influence the granting of access, including organizational structures, IT systems, access levels, and data elements.

There is, however, a *correct time* to build roles. We highly recommend starting this phase later in the Identity Governance program, so you can leverage the knowledge you've gained, and reap the benefits from more accurate assignment data. At this point in the program process, your organization will likely have completed several cycles of access reviews, removing outdated and incorrect accesses in the process. Performing comparative analysis of access (role mining), from a solid validated data foundation, is essential to the creation of meaningful roles.

Your organization will have gained knowledge about the accesses the organization already has in "the current state," which can be used to improve descriptions for access review or access request processes. Building upon this familiarity will help you shape the roles in your organization. We recommend starting with roles and areas of concern that are most familiar to the business. Areas of common access or high turnover (e.g., retail or call centers) are generally great places to start, as the access assigned there is aligned with traditional provisioning or deprovisioning cycles.

Another way to gain familiarity with access is by analyzing the trends and behavior seen in the access request phase. Commonly requested and granted access might indicate that these access models can effectively be mapped to new enterprise roles. This allows commonly requested access to be moved to automated role assignment tasks instead.

With role-based access control, it is also very tempting to attempt to deliver *all roles, for the entire organization, all at once*. Defining fine-grained access via a role model can be a complex understating. Attempting this process on an organization-wide basis can further complicate the process. Instead, it's better to start with well-understood, coarse-grained accesses and work your way toward more fine-grained access as the process iterates over time and access patterns are better understood.

Very few customers who elect to deploy roles in a "big bang" project approach are truly successful. We therefore strongly recommend starting small and iterating. Role definitions are rarely set in stone and therefore are best left to evolve over time in sync with your changing business, IT, and security posture. Leverage your intrinsic knowledge, start small and iterate.

6. Separation of Duty (SoD)

- ***Project Goal*** – *Implement detective controls, based on access roles and entitlements*

- ***Program Objective*** – *Leverage existing controls to detect fine-grained access controls.*

Separation of duty (SoD) enables you to put controls in place and to monitor and guarantee that your organization continues to meet key audit and compliance requirements. While implementing separation of duty is not technically complex, it does require cooperative knowledge from audit teams and a good understanding of business process controls in your organization. We therefore recommend waiting until your Identity Governance program has settled, access data is understood, key sources are onboarded, and major controls and governance features are implemented before defining SoD controls.

7. Password Management

- ***Project Goal*** – *Deliver self-service password reset and "forgot my password" features.*

- ***Program Objective*** – *Deliver a quick win establishing an identity-based paradigm, while simultaneously reducing the overhead of help desk calls.*

Password management is a relatively straightforward deployment, delivering almost immediate value back to the business by reducing the pain and cost of password reset calls made through the help desk. Password management focuses on self-service password reset and "forgot my password" workflows to reset passwords. To change several passwords at once, passwords can be grouped into password sync groups, enabling "same sign-on" where single sign-on (SSO) may not be entirely feasible.

Password management can be deployed at any time, within any of the other phases. Some customers prefer to implement it early on, as a "quick win" for the business, which may be crucial to getting their program up and running.

CHAPTER 13

Privileged Access Management

Privileged Access Management (PAM) is a subdiscipline within the Identity Governance framework. The PAM universe can be implemented and operate on its own or be integrated into an organization's Identity Access Management (IAM) program. Figure 13-1 illustrates IAM at a high level and all of the potential technology and security disciplines included in the framework.

© Morey J. Haber, Darran Rolls 2020
M. J. Haber and D. Rolls, *Identity Attack Vectors*, https://doi.org/10.1007/978-1-4842-5165-2_13

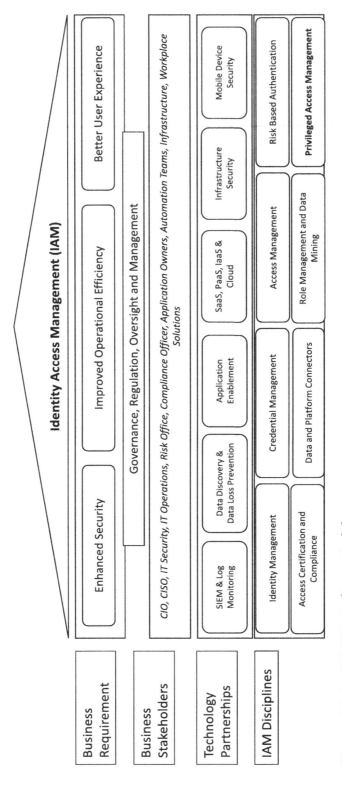

Figure 13-1. *IAM Disciplines Model*

Organizations may choose to start with either an Identity Governance (IG) or PAM implementation in order to meet their objectives; however, unifying both should be their ultimate goal as they mature through the IAM lifecycle. In fairness, many organizations will never mature to this point, but the goal should always remain to streamline the identity and security process.

By definition, PAM is a methodology to secure, control, monitor, and manage privileged activity to resources. The discipline includes multiple components to manage privileged identities, accounts, and credentials and their corresponding passwords, certificates, and keys. The objective of PAM is to lower risk by only providing privileged access to users and resources that need administrative or root privileges to complete a task or mission. This helps remove or eliminate privileges from common day operations. This then forms the basis for a least privilege account model.

The resources under PAM management can include anything from an operating system to applications, databases, network devices, scripts, DevOps, IoT, cloud resources, and so on. It is a universe of subdisciplines. The implementation of PAM is performed using dedicated solutions, policies, and procedures that focus on managing privileges and all the locations where they may be present. IAM solutions interface with PAM by managing and certifying the identities associated with PAM accounts and credentials using an integrated Identity Governance solution.

PAM solutions provide organizations the secure privileged access tools needed to protect all assets regardless of where they are situated and typically focus on the critical resources containing the most sensitive information and infrastructure.

As previously stated, not all identities and accounts associated with an Identity should be included in a PAM model. PAM focuses on identities and accounts that are used for privileged access. Whether those are administrators, root, or superusers does not matter. The only time PAM typically includes non-privileged accounts is when the credentials need to be under management for access. This is typically the case for technology like remote access solutions (secure remote access is covered further in Chapter 17). These could be either privileged or non-privileged accounts that require password management for compliance and security and the automatic retrieval and rotation of passwords to manage risks.

To understand all of the capabilities of PAM, please refer to Figure 13-2, Privileged Access Management components and the universe of components required for a complete implementation.

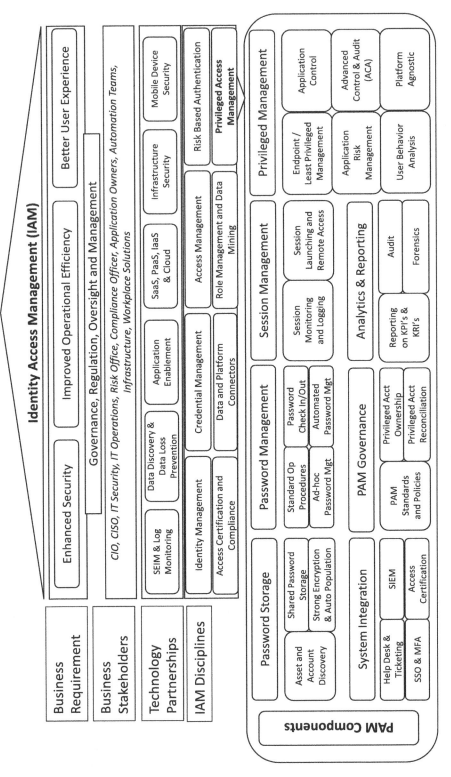

Figure 13-2. *Privileged Access Management (PAM) components*

An enterprise-class PAM solution usually consists of the following components:

- **Password Storage** – The ability of a solution to securely store or vault credentials and accounts in a password safe for manual, automatic, or programmatic retrieval by an identity.

    - **Asset and Account Discovery** – The capability of a tool or process to identify assets connected to a network and all the accounts, privileged or not, allowed to function on the resource and their associated privileges and group membership.

    - **Shared Password Storage** – Security best practices dictate that only one identity should have access to an account and its associated password. However, many technology implementations do not support proper Role-Based Access Controls (RBACs), and a single account needs to be used by multiple people. For example, a resource may only allow one administrator account, but there are multiple administrators in an organization that need access to the resource. Therefore, shared password storage is a use case expansion of password storage to allow a one-to-many approach for account access.

    - **Strong Encryption and Auto-population** – Any password that is stored should be encrypted against potential theft by a threat actor. In addition, any exposure or transmission over the network of the password should also be encrypted regardless of its use case and implementation. This includes automatic password injection technology and automatic password population technology that may provide a seamless user experience and protect the password from human or third-party machine-readable exposure, such as memory-scraping malware.

- **Password Management** – The ability to perform management functions on a password associated with an account. This includes password changes across human and non-human accounts such as service accounts, applications, and even scripts.

- **Standard Operating Procedures (SOPs)** – Many organizations have a standard password management policy. This can include the complexity of the password and the required frequency of rotation for the password. These policies must be electronically translatable into a PAM solution and form the basis for automated password management.

- **Ad Hoc Password Management** – While password management is typically considered an automated process, there are occasions that ad hoc password management is required. These can include as follows:

  - **Break Glass** – A security or operational exception requiring manual password management of retrieval

  - **Incident or Breach** – The manual forcing of password management changes across potentially a large quantity of accounts outside of SOP

  - **Employee or Human Resources Request** – The manual changing of passwords associated with an identity due to an employee life event

  Ad hoc password management adheres to the policies in your SOP but allows for them to be enforced or altered to mitigate an out-of-bounds threat or emergency situation. It is important to note all ad hoc request types should be documented in your SOPs, but managed ad hoc since their potential usage and cycle is not predictable.

- **Password Check In/Out** – The ability to validate an identity based on credentials for the retrieval of a password and, subsequently, check them back in once their usage is complete.

- **Automated Password Management** – The programmatic rotation of passwords, certificates, or keys based on policies implemented in the PAM solution that align with the organization's SOP for password management.

- **Session Management** – The ability of the PAM solution to record user or application interaction with a command or remote session regardless of connection protocol and index the activity on screen or through the keyboard or mouse for future searching, retrieval, and forensics.

    - **Session Monitoring and Logging** – The ability to document session activity for human auditing in real time or at a later date and, in addition, the ability to log activity in machine-readable formats for log consolidation, user behavior analytics, or event correlation to determine indicator of compromise (IoC).

    - **Session Launching** – The ability to automatically launch a session, including injecting the credentials automatically and managing the connection for duration, contents, data loss, and commands.

- **Privilege Management** – The ability to monitor, control, and terminate any and all privileged activity occurring on a resource, whether by user or application.

    - **Endpoint Least Privilege Management** – The ability to enforce a least privilege user model on any endpoint regardless of server, workstation, or infrastructure. User and application privileges are minimized to the lowest denominator in order to perform a task or mission, and, when higher privileges are required, the application, resource, or operating system function is elevated without the end user or application explicitly entering elevated credentials.

    - **Application Risk Management** – Applications, even from trusted vendors, can have a wide variety of risks based on their configuration and known vulnerabilities. Application risk management assesses the risk of the application before applying privileged access in order to mitigate any known threats. This concept is typically called Reputation-Based Services or Vulnerability-Based Application management (VBAM) and includes context-aware services to the application to determine its origin before execution.

- **User Behavior Analysis (UBA)** – A user may execute certain applications and operating system tasks in a rather repeatable fashion based on their role and job functions. In addition, some applications and commands should never be executed together, like access to sensitive data and a screen sharing application or file transfer program. User behavior analysis builds a model based on activity and will send an event or create an alert when suspicious behavior is occurring or when known threat patterns match an identity's electronic behavior.

- **Application Control** – The ability to affect the runtime of an application on a resource based on any criteria the solution can quantify. This includes techniques like whitelisting, blacklisting, and even graylisting applications to execute (with or without privileges) based on environment, vendor, geolocation, download source, and so on. Typically, organizations will blacklist a specific vendor or classes of tools, like bit torrents, since they have no licenses and lack legitimate business purposes within an organization.

- **Advanced Control and Audit (ACA)** – While command filtering is the primary method most vendors use for privilege management, it does not take into consideration renamed applications and commands potentially embedded in scripts. Using agent or client-based technology, ACA allows for command filtering below what a user types in and is visible on the screen. It can perform application control on commands hidden from plain sight and monitors how commands interact with applications and the operating system to block potentially malicious activity that has been obfuscated from session monitoring. Many times, this can be in the form of child processes or intentionally altering scripts to perform additional, potentially malicious, activities.

- **Platform-Agnostic** – Privileged management translates to every platform. It is agnostic. Whether the device is Windows, MacOS, Unix, Linux, IoT, DevOps, Cloud, Virtual, Router, Switch, or any other infrastructure, the concepts of privilege management apply to all of them. A PAM solution should be able to address every aspect of your organization where privileged access is used.

- **System Integration** – Every solution licensed and installed in your environment should integrate in some form with the rest of your operational and security ecosystem. For PAM and IAM, the following are critical to the success of your implementation.

  - **Helpdesk and Ticketing** – Privileged access should follow an established workflow and approval process. The integration into existing ticketing systems, call centers, and help desk solutions allows for a documented workflow and approval process to grant or deny access and verify identities before granting privileged access to resources. In other words, a support ticket must be opened, or is dynamically created, and approved (even if self-approved), before privileged activity can occur on any resource.

  - **Single Sign-On (SSO) and Multifactor Authentication (MFA)** – Based on privileged attack vectors and identity attack vectors, privileged authentication should not rely on credentials requiring only a username and password combination. In fact, even systems that are moderately sensitive but accessible to the end user should use SSO and/or MFA to secure access. This will prevent password reuse, credential stuffing, and a variety of other attack vectors that could allow escalation of privileges and a threat actor owning an identity.

  - **Security Information and Event Management (SIEM)** – It is an approach to security management that aggregates security information and event management information into a single platform. The data can be analyzed, filtered, and correlated and have artificial intelligence engines applied to the results to look for anomalies and other indicators of compromise. All PAM events from password retrievals, session launches, and password changes should be sent to a SIEM for processing as a part of your larger security management program.

- **Access Certification** – Identity Governance solutions provide certification reports that detail who could have access to a resource. PAM solutions provide certification reports on who accessed a resource and what they did with that access. Most auditors, based on regulatory compliance requirements, will want to see both.

- **Privileged Access Management (PAM) Governance** – While PAM is a discipline based on the management of administrator and root privileges, the governance of PAM focuses on the policies and procedures required by an organization to actually implement it in day-to-day operations.

  - **PAM Standards and Policies** – Outside of the standard operating procedures (SOPs) used for password management covered in the preceding text, PAM standards and policies must also govern who should have access, when they should have access, and what privileges should they be delegated. Not every information technology administrator should have administrative rights to every resource. Therefore, the governance aspects of PAM detail all the aspects of privileges and when they should be assigned or revoked from different identities. This granularity goes far beyond a password complexity policy and typically leverages the Role assignments in IAM to properly implement.

  - **Privileged Account Ownership** – As previously defined, every identity can have multiple accounts. Some identities are human and some electronic. The ownership of every account should be clearly defined and documented as a part of your processes. A PAM implementation can help document this correlation for privileged accounts.

  - **Privileged Account Reconciliation** – Organizations change and so do employees, as well as does the ownership of projects, technology, and resources. Privileged account reconciliation is a cumulative process that uses all aspects of PAM from discovery to privileged application usage through privileged account ownership, to verify all aspects are operating according to plan. For example, if an application has a policy to allow users to elevate an application for administrative usage, and the application is no longer being used, the privileged account reconciliation process should identify an obsolete rule. Then, the proper teams can flag it for change control and remove it from the affected policies. This PAM component is typically implemented using reports based on live privileged usage data compared to implemented policies for privileged access within the PAM solution.

- **Analytics and Reporting**

    - **Reporting on Key Performance Indicators (KPIs) and Key Risk Indicators (KRIs)** – Any information and security solution implemented within an environment should be able to produce reports, alerts, and events to indicate the health of the environment, as well as to quantify performance and risk. It is a self-reporting model. How well are you managing privileges, are there deviations in risk that need attention, and is the overall performance acceptable by end users and applications to meet business objectives?

    - **Audit** – Regulatory compliance and internal auditors will want reporting on privileged activity regardless of where it is conducted. A PAM solution should be able to generate a wide variety of audit reports to satisfy these requirements in real time and from historical access.

    - **Forensics** – The data generated from a PAM solution is invaluable for determining indicators of compromise and for forensics investigations. A PAM solution should be able to deliver granular reports for items like an application hash, command-line switches, and runtime patch in order to satisfy these requirements.

With all these in mind, PAM also has industry standard acronyms to help group and explain these disciplines. Vendors rarely license them individually, and organizations will typically reference their solutions in these categories to meet their requirements:

- **Account Password Management (APM)** – APM provides a technology approach to securely manage privileged credentials, including system accounts, service accounts, cloud accounts, and application accounts. APM solutions use strong encryption and a hardened password safe for storing passwords, keys, and other privileged credentials, for a controlled, audited, and policy-driven release and update.

- **Privileged Account and Session Management (PASM)** – Privileged accounts are protected by storing or vaulting their credentials in a password safe. Access to those accounts is managed by a PASM solution for all resources, including human users, services, and applications. Passwords and other credentials for privileged accounts are placed under management, and passwords can be rotated (changed) at definable intervals or upon occurrence of specific events – such as the end of a session or when an IAM solution triggers a significant personnel change (e.g., a key individual being terminated) or an incident with accounts being compromised.

- **Privileged Session Management (PSM)** – Session management establishes a remote connection to a resource manually or automatically through credential injection and provides session recording.

- **Session Recording and Monitoring (SRM)** – SRM provides additional capabilities to PSM tools that offer advanced auditing, monitoring, active management, and review of privileged activities during a privileged session. This includes but is certainly not limited to

  - Key-stroke logging and indexing for searchable content

  - Video session recording and playback at various speeds

  - Screen scraping with indexing with search capabilities

  - OCR translation of graphical screens

- **Application-to-Application Password Management (AAPM)** – This is also referred to A2A PASM. It provides the ability for application resources, typically through a REST API, to integrate into a password management and storage solution with a high fidelity of security and encryption.

- **Privilege Elevation and Delegation Management (PEDM)** – Specific privileges are granted on the managed resource and can be controlled by identity, account, or credentials and are context aware. The resource can be a server, workstation, mobile device, IoT, or infrastructure. Once a user or application authenticates to the resource, commands and applications are elevated based on tasks or mission – without necessarily requiring an explicit input of the privileged account. This technology includes host-based command control (filtering) that can be implemented without the use of local agents or local privileged elevation which requires a locally installed client to elevate the application, perform a RunAs or SuDo, or use AAPM to retrieve a valid credential.

- **User Behavior Analytics (UBA)** – UBA uses data analytics to detect threats based on anomalous behavior and established rules and behavioral profiles. The results are designed to be correlated with other security solutions to determine intent and potential indicators of compromise.

All of the preceding components, as a universe of PAM disciplines, can be managed by an IAM solution to standardize privileged account entitlements and provide certifications for who or what has privileged rights. PAM via PASM and PSM then provides the compliance reporting for the actual activity that has occurred. The goal is to provide true visibility into what an identity is allowed to do and what their associated accounts actually performed – whether malicious or legitimate. The solution should identity whether the behavior was appropriate or inappropriate – and ultimately reveal indicators of compromise based on privileged or identity-based attack vectors. Figure 13-3 illustrates this synergy.

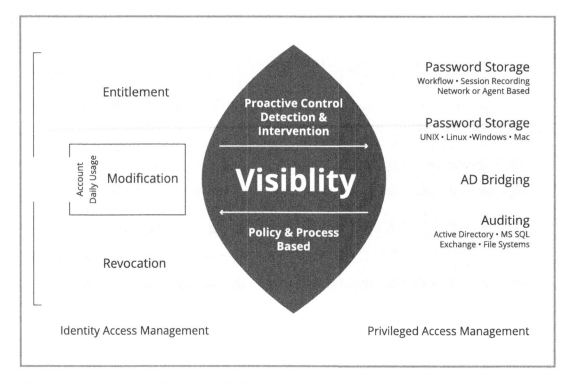

Figure 13-3. *IAM and PAM visibility*

This forms the basis for any threat investigation against an identity and associated account by linking IAM and PAM for forensics and establishes ownership for the who, what, when, how, and where. This completes the necessary information when determining a threat based on the privileged attack chain and the cyber kill chain.

CHAPTER 14

Just-in-Time Access Management

The concept of Just-in-Time (JIT) Access Management is a strategy that aligns real-time requests for usage of accounts directly with entitlements without the static assignment of an account or privilege to an Identity. Companies use this strategy to secure accounts from continuous real-time access by restricting them based on appropriate behavior, context, and other ephemeral properties. This decreases the risk of an always-on account that can be leveraged by a threat actor outside of acceptable use policies and procedures. This method requires organizations to establish criteria for just-in-time access and accept that these accounts are not available outside of potentially break glass scenarios.

Although similar concepts for JIT in the manufacturing space are well established, using the model for a security and operations solutions does present some interesting technical considerations during implementation. The first is around the just-in-time account delegated for access. An account is granted entitlements, privileges, and permissions only when it is actually needed for usage. Most of the time, this is a privileged account and is commonly an administrator account or some special account based on some form of ITSM exception. The goal of a JIT account is to assign the necessary privileges "on the fly" based on an approved task or approval workflow and subsequently remove them once the task is complete or the window or context for authorized access is expired.

© Morey J. Haber, Darran Rolls 2020
M. J. Haber and D. Rolls, *Identity Attack Vectors*, https://doi.org/10.1007/978-1-4842-5165-2_14

The modeling required to take an account and apply the appropriate privileges can be implemented using the following JIT techniques:

- **JIT Account Creation and Deletion** – The creation and deletion of an appropriate account to meet mission objectives. The account should have traits to link it back to the requesting identity or service performing the operation for logging and forensics. Connectors in the Identity Governance layer can typically manage this requirement.

- **JIT Group Membership** – The automatic addition and removal of an account into a privileged administrative group for the duration of the mission. The account should only be added in an elevated group when the appropriate criteria are met and subsequently removed when the mission is complete. Again connectors in the IG layer typically manage these group membership requests as part of a normal entitlement modeling and service provisioning process.

- **JIT Entitlement** – The account has individual privileges, permissions, or entitlements added to perform a mission but only for a limited duration once all criteria are met. These rights need to be revoked once the mission is complete and should include certification that no other privileges were inappropriately altered. These can be managed by connections between the Identity Governance and PAM Solution, or to target application.

- **JIT Delegation** – The account is linked to a preexisting administrative account(s), and when a specific application or task is performed, the function is elevated using those credentials. This is commonly done using automation or scripting with Windows "RunAs" or *Nix SuDo. Typically, the end user is not aware of the impersonation account for this type of operation and may overlap with always-on privileged account delegation. This is typically done only with the integration into a PAM solution.

- **JIT Disabled Administrative Accounts** – Disabled administrator accounts are present in a system with all the permissions, privileges, and entitlements to perform a function. They are enabled to perform a specific mission and then subsequently disabled again once operational criteria have been satisfied. This concept is no different than having always-on administrative accounts except native enablement functionality is leveraged to control JIT access. This functionality can be achieved by either the Identity Governance system or the PAM endpoint privileged management solution if available.

- **JIT Tokenization** – The application or resource has its privileged token modified before injection into the operating system kernel. This form of least privilege is commonly used on endpoints to elevate the privileges and priority of an application and not the end users themselves. This technology is the cornerstone for endpoint privileged management for PAM solutions.

For any of these account privileges and entitlements to occur just in time, the following criteria should be considered as triggers. These should also include variables like time and date for change control windows and suspension or termination criteria if indicators of compromise are detected.

- **Entitlements** – When privileged access management is integrated with camel case, entitlements between the solutions can be synchronized for privileged access. To that end, JIT access can be assigned via PAM solutions directly or through dynamic entitlements provisioning. While the Identity Governance entitlement workflow can sometimes be a longer technology process, it does provide a means of greater control and oversight and again can be best achieved by linking IG with PAM via vendor-supplied integration.

- **Workflow** – The concept of workflow approvals is commonly associated with call centers, help desks, and the identity provisioning control layer. A request is made for access, and using a defined workflow process, interactive approval is sought from the appropriate approver or owner and access is either granted or denied. With approvals and audit in hand, a JIT account can be enabled. This typically corresponds to the user, asset, application, time/date, and associated ticket in a change control or help desk solution.

- **Context-Aware** – Context-aware access is based on criteria like source IP address, geolocation, group membership, host operating system, applications installed or operating in memory, documented vulnerabilities, and so on. Based on any logical combination of these traits, JIT account access can be granted or revoked in order to satisfy business requirements and mitigate risk.

- **Two-Factor (2FA) or Multifactor Authentication (MFA)** – A common method for authorizing privileged access to always-on or JIT privileged accounts is 2FA or MFA. While this does not distinguish between the two access techniques, it does provide additional risk mitigation in assuring the identity does have proper access to a privileged account. It can, however, be used as a JIT trigger for an account using any of the techniques listed here.

JIT triggers are just that, conditions for an account to be placed in a temporary just-in-time state. They can be used standalone or logically grouped with other triggers to instantiate privileged account access. The key takeaway for teams to consider is what policies govern a JIT account for proper access and what conditions should be met for its revocation? These could include

- Time and date windows for access and change control

- Commands or applications that may indicate a compromising event

- Detection of access to sensitive information

- Termination of the primary session

- Existence of corresponding collateral in a ticketing solution

- Inappropriate modification of resources including installing software or modifying files

- Inappropriate attempts at lateral movement

- The manipulation, creation, or deletion of user accounts or datasets

While this is not an exhaustive list, it can help filter the criteria for a JIT account to be made available based on corresponding triggers.

While Just-in-Time (JIT) Access Management is not a new concept, the utilization of always-on accounts has been the primary vehicle for administrative access for the last 40 years. The risk of always-on accounts, unfortunately, is expanding. New highly entitled and privileged accounts are required for virtual, cloud, IoT, and DevOps environments in order to administer solutions. The quantity and location create complexity. And this complexity, in turn, often translates into increased risks around security, operational continuity, and compliance. Traditional perimeter-based security technologies only can protect privileged accounts within their boundaries. Privileged accounts are now truly everywhere. Each of them is potentially another privileged and identity attack vector, and some of them are accessible directly on the Internet. This is where integrating JIT Access Management with Identity Governance can make a significant difference in securing your environment from identity attack vectors.

CHAPTER 15

Identity Obfuscation

In this age of identity attack vectors, protecting one's identity cannot be done stand-alone. There are plenty of opportunities for a threat actor to steal your identity using the very information technology that we embrace every day. We have covered that in detail in previous chapters. However, there is another mitigation approach called Privacy Filters that can limit a threat actor's ability to create that critical linkage between account, identity, and data and craft identity obfuscation.

Privacy Filters are typically application features, dedicated software, or even physical additions to devices to shield your data and protect your identity. They are required by law in some cases (e.g., GDPR) to obfuscate a user's identity in order to collect performance and analytic data. They can have far-reaching ramifications in the form of financial penalties if they breach regulatory compliance requirements for data and identity collection. And, they can shield your identity from many physical and electronic threats a threat actor may utilize to gain an advantage. Consider the following Privacy Filters:

- **Incognito Browsing Mode (Private Browsing)** – The ability of a web-based browser to block cookies, browser version information, history data, and other sensitive information that could be used to determine your persona and identity or even launch a targeted attack based on runtime data submitted by your computer during the course of a browsing session.

- **Identity Obfuscation** – The ability for software to collect performance, analytic, event, and support information and automatically scrub it for personally identifiable information about the user, applications, or even environment before submitting to a vendor or installed solution. This type of technology is typically used to protect data from being sent over a regional or country boundary when data privacy laws prohibit a company or organization from storing or sending it with granular identity information.

157

© Morey J. Haber, Darran Rolls 2020
M. J. Haber and D. Rolls, *Identity Attack Vectors*, https://doi.org/10.1007/978-1-4842-5165-2_15

- **Screen Privacy Filters** – These are physical polarized filters added to computer screens to prevent threat actors from viewing a screen from obtuse angles. A user can clearly see the screen when operating directly in front of it or from very small angles off a perpendicular axis. This is designed to stop shoulder surfing and the errand linkage of information that could be present on a user's machine and visible to inappropriate users.

- **Guest Shopping Carts** – While not directly considered a privacy filter, allowing the purchasing of items anonymously by an online retailer (or using a guest account) is a form of a privacy filter. The user's identity is restricted to the transaction, and an account, with detailed identity information, is not stored for future use. This reduces the risk of an identity account by not having an account created in a potentially untrustworthy retailer. For frequent online shoppers, using a guest account for shopping is highly recommended for merchants that you infrequently (or one time) visit.

Therefore, depending on your organization's requirements, you may consider implementing privacy filters in order to minimize risk and meet regulatory compliance requirements. For example, information technology owners may install computer-based privacy filters on all laptops to prevent data leakage as employees travel or on desktops in a financial institution to limit privileged information. Security teams may request data obfuscation on Windows Events Logs for a solution to prevent identity information from showing up in a SIEM. And businesses may use guest accounts on operating systems to allow many-to-one usage of computing devices vs. creating accounts for every identity in order to save costs. While this last use case may sound extreme, many applications are licensed by user, and if the data can be represented in a generic nonsensitive fashion, then protecting someone's identity (by not making an account) can have profound outcomes in lowering cost too.

Privacy filters and other forms of obfuscation technology can help mitigate the threats of identity attack vectors. If you consider every place an identity may be exposed, other solutions may be available to obfuscate it from reporting, management, and collection without diminishing the mission at hand.

CHAPTER 16

System for Cross-Domain Identity Management (SCIM)

System for Cross-Domain Identity Management (SCIM) is a standard for automating the exchange of user identity information between identity domains, identity-based solutions, and participating information technology resources. SCIM uses a standardized REST API and data formatted in JSON or XML to allow interoperating solutions to exchange information in a standardized way. The standard simplifies the methodology for provisioning and deprovisioning (cradle to grave) of an identity and associated accounts such that customized and proprietary connectors are not necessary to exchange information.

A real-world example would flow as follows: consider an organization provisions new employees and, at a later, date terminates them. This could easily be a temporary employee, contractor, or even a team member that changes job functions. As they are added and removed from the company's electronic employee directory (Active Directory, LDAP, etc.), SCIM could be used to automatically create or delete (provision or deprovision) accounts for those users in other applications and share the information with other tools, such as a privileged access management solution. Ergo, a new or modified user account would be synchronized automatically for each employee using a standard protocol, and the user accounts for terminated employees would be automatically removed avoiding the potential risks associated with identities and accounts not removed from an organization. Figure 16-1 illustrates this process applied to the integration between elements of the IAM ecosystem.

© Morey J. Haber, Darran Rolls 2020
M. J. Haber and D. Rolls, *Identity Attack Vectors*, https://doi.org/10.1007/978-1-4842-5165-2_16

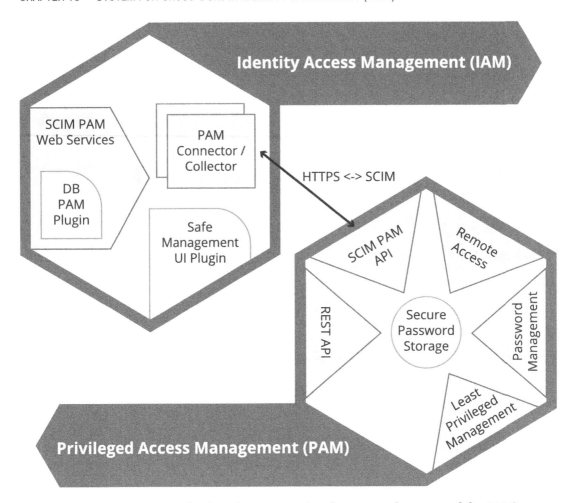

Figure 16-1. *Process applied to the integration between elements of the IAM ecosystem*

In addition to standardized account record management (creating and deleting), SCIM can also be used to share information about user attributes, attribute schema, and group and role membership. Identity attributes can contain contact information to group membership applied to an account. Group membership and other attributes are generally used to manage user permissions using other solutions, like privileged access management. These values and group assignments are designed to change based on employment and environmental conditions, and SCIM provides a vehicle to synchronize this information across multiple managed domains, or directly within applications, whether on premise or in the cloud.

The benefits of SCIM are elementary. The standard has grown in expectance, and organizations can save hundreds of man-hours in provisioning and deprovisioning accounts across systems manually while also avoiding the potential pitfalls of manual human provisioning. In contrast, without a standard connection method, companies must write custom software connectors to manage these accounts across proprietary systems. This simple condition is what creates the value for most IAM vendors since they have hundreds of connectors to manage non-SCIM-compliant resources.

CHAPTER 17

Remote Access

One of the challenges for remote access technology is providing role-based access to groups and individuals outside of your organization. Their assets are essentially untrusted, and their accounts often fall outside of your control. They are essentially foreign entities that need validation and authentication before any connection or remote session can occur. This typically occurs for vendors and contractors that need remote access into your environment, but there is no directory service or authoritative store that can be established using a connector to manage a user's identity and associated accounts.

If an organization attempts to provide authentication based on an unmanaged account alone, the risk is typically unacceptable to the business. Organizations customarily create domain accounts for these identities so they can authenticate against the domain, and their account is placed under management. This creates an interesting dilemma. The identity of the user has accounts and credentials that are managed by the organization, but they are not employees of the organization. Your relationship with them is not trusted, and the assets being used by both may not be under your management control for cybersecurity hygiene best practices. Perhaps you have a split management model and only control the account itself. This warrants abstracting technologies like remote access to a higher level using the user's identity and not just a proxy account in your domain. The question is how to accomplish this goal?

Regardless of how you carve it up, the end user will still need an account to initiate connectivity. Whether you create the account in your domain or not may be a matter of your own security policy rather than the risk itself. The risk manifests itself in the access control, source of the connection, and connection and network connectivity required by the account. For example, does the remote access connection require

- Connectivity via VPN client
- Protocol-based tunneling for RDP, SSH, or other dedicated applications

© Morey J. Haber, Darran Rolls 2020
M. J. Haber and D. Rolls, *Identity Attack Vectors*, https://doi.org/10.1007/978-1-4842-5165-2_17

- Connecting through a NAC solution for asset health checks

- Conforming to acceptable use stands for applications and security for remote applications

- Using a dedicated secure remote access technology

- A remote browser or dedicated "fat-client" software to be installed remotely for the mission to succeed

In each of these scenarios, the account may be trusted, but the asset (host) may not be trusted unless the device is issued by the organization. For someone like a contractor, remote employee, or vendor, odds are that the device is managed by someone else and validation of threats for the supply chain is an exercise in policy rather than technology. Therefore, the first step is to consider the account used for authentication. It should be under the control of the Identity Governance system and should have a real employee as the owner. Then make sure an account exists to manage a connected device as a potentially high-risk asset. Mitigation should start at the identity level and propagate down to all related accounts and entitlements. An example of an indicator of compromise here might be the ability to measure when more than one account is used by the same identity at the same time.

Remote access technologies can be deployed via the cloud and on premise or built on top of existing tools like VPN and RDP. In order to mitigate identity attack vectors, based on the three-pillar model, organizations should mitigate the risks from the asset and provide connectivity strictly by an account and with a least privilege model.

To accomplish this goal, a remote access solution must be compatible with the roles and privileges in your Identity Governance implementation. This assigns the appropriate account the entitlements to start a remote session only for the appropriate targets. Next, the remote session tool must abstract usage of a resource to the lowest common dominator for risk. This typically is a web browser, and, if a remote access technology can make any and all sessions available through a web browser, then an identity can be abstracted since there is only one connection type available.

This approach to identity-based remote access is only found in vendors that integrate remote access and Identity Governance as a single solution. The goal is to link access from the "external" account to the identity for the user accessing resources. If you are looking for the simplest explanation for this approach, remote access, whether on premise, cloud, or external, should use a governance-based approach for management and control of access in order to mitigate the risks of the connecting asset. There is no way to know what resources have access to that account, especially if the asset connecting is not under your control. It could be a threat actor, trusted individual, untrusted computing device, and other combinations. If you take a governance-based approach, the user is managed by their identity, at a layer above the account, and access is granted by the Identity Governance system and remote access solution working together. A PAM solution can provide an additional layer of control by restricting access to these privileges. In the end, you can always provide an access review for who should have access and can always determine if the activity was appropriate, regardless of source, using a session monitoring tool.

CHAPTER 18

Identity-Based Threat Response

No one wants to respond to a security incident or a breach. There is never a good time for a breach. Instead, the highest priority should always be to stop a cyberthreat *before* it compromises the organization.

In reality, preventing a cyberattack from happening in the first place is not always possible. In fact, almost every organization suffers from security incidents on a fairly regular basis these days. The steps for an incident or breach identification, from threat hunting to searching for explicit IoC, are well established. While the processes will vary from organization to organization, malware, compromised identities, lateral movement, data exfiltration, and so on will all need to be addressed as a part of any post-incident cleanup plan.

If a breach is severe enough (e.g., including the compromise of servers and domain controllers), organizations may have no choice other than to reinstall the entire environment from scratch. While this is a worst-case scenario, it does happen. In many cases, businesses may choose to scrub servers as best as possible vs. performing a complete reinstall – a business decision to be made based on the risk, feasibility, and cost. It also represents a no-win scenario if the threat is a persistent presence that uses techniques to evade traditional identification measures. If you think that is far-fetched, just look at the history of threats like rootkits, Spectra, and Meltdown that each provide a way to persistently attack a technology resource. In the end, threat actors are after your identities and their associated credentials, and they all too frequently succeed.

Regardless of your prevention strategy, you can be assured that, in the end, via some means or another, threat actors will have access to your credentials and potentially much more. This implies that any cleanup effort should not reuse existing identities, credentials, accounts, passwords, or keys linked to the breach. In fact, it should be

© Morey J. Haber, Darran Rolls 2020
M. J. Haber and D. Rolls, *Identity Attack Vectors*, https://doi.org/10.1007/978-1-4842-5165-2_18

considered a best practice to rotate/reset all credentials across all affected or linked resource – even if they have not been directly associated with usage by the threat actor in the specific incident.

This is where Identity Governance and PAM solutions can help after a breach or an incident. Using the automation and self-service capabilities outlined in the preceding text, you can help prevent identity, account, credential, and password reuse. By creating a system-based approach to the tracking, managing, and resetting of access, we can greatly reduce the time to mitigation and reduce the impact to users and business processes.

With this in mind, consider the following steps for your remediation plan:

- **Forensics:**

  - Isolate which identities were compromised and link them to ALL associated accounts, whether used by a human or machine. This is a forensics exercise, and not all accounts may be affected. This access can then be reset by the Identity Governance or PAM solution depending on where the privileges reside.

  - Determine which accounts were actually compromised and used for access and lateral movement. These should be deleted and recreated. Often, just resetting the password alone is not good enough, especially if the threat actor has compromised the SID or changed the login profile scripts or login execution path.

  - Determine the resources compromised by these accounts and any linkage. For example, the same account that was compromised on asset X or application Y is also used on assets A, B, and C for applications D, E, and F so they can all communicate.

  - Identify any illicit identities and accounts created by the threat actor. An access-based review and account reconciliation report will help with this task.

  - Analyze how data was used/accessed by the attacker during the breach. Was any IoC data captured during the abuse of the privileged account? If data was captured, did it help to identify the threat? If data was not captured, determine what needs to change to monitor future misuse of accounts or privileges. This includes privileged account usage as well as session monitoring and keystroke logging, where appropriate.

- **Remediation:**

  - Purge any rogue identities and accounts created by the threat actor.

  - Remove or segment any shadow IT, IoT, or other resources that were part of the cyberattack chain, to protect against future threats using lateral movement.

  - Determine the least amount of privileges needed for each account to perform their functions. Most users and system accounts do not require full domain or local administrator or root accounts, and your mitigation plan should apply the appropriate identity access management roles to the accounts to minimize risk.

Be warned; this analysis is not trivial, and you may need third-party help to perform these tasks. It is a forgone conclusion that tools will be needed to help discover compromised accounts, to identify changed resources, to determine unusual usage patterns, and, most importantly, to flag any potential abuse of privilege. Even if all available log and usage data is sent to a SIEM, it still requires the correlation or user behavior analytics to answer these questions. Next-generation Identity Governance solutions that include AI and ML technology can help to identify these threats earlier in the detection cycle and throughout the forensic and remediation process.

Once you have made the initial investigation, here are the five ways Identity Governance and PAM solutions can help after a breach and that should be considered an essential component of your cleanup efforts:

1. After a discovery, automatically onboard accounts that may have been identified that were not a part of your known-state Identity Governance model. The goal is to get them under management quickly and efficiently. Based on established policies, enforce unique and complex passwords with automatic rotation for each using the PAM system. This will help ensure any persistent presence cannot repeatedly leverage compromised credentials.

2. For any linked accounts, check usage information and, if necessary, rotate passwords, keys, and certificates altogether on a periodic schedule, including where possible your service accounts. This will keep the accounts synchronized and potentially isolated from other forms of password reuse.

3. When applicable, remove unnecessary privileged accounts all the way down to the desktop. This includes any secondary accounts associated with an identity. For any application, command, or task that requires administrative rights, consider the least privilege model that elevates the application – not the user – to perform privileged management.

4. Using your Identity Governance and PAM infrastructure, look for IoCs that suggest lateral movement, either from commands or rogue user behavior. This is a critical portion of the cyberkill chain where these tools can help identify whether or not any resources have been compromised.

5. Application control is one of the best defenses against malware. This capability includes looking for trusted applications that are vulnerable to threats by leveraging various forms of reputation-based services. Identity Governance and PAM can help here too. Decide on an application's runtime based on trust and known risks before it is allowed to interact with the user, data, network, and operating system.

Identity access management and privileged access management should be considered for new projects and legacy systems to stop identity and privilege attack vectors. It should also be considered for forensics and remediation control after an incident since it is potentially the lowest hanging fruit within your organization that links a threat actor to the identity compromised for mal-intent.

Therefore, as a security best practice, identity and privileged access should always be linked and used as an integrated solution. When a threat actor gains administrator or root credentials, they do have the keys to your kingdom. The goal is to stop them from obtaining them and owning compromised accounts.

CHAPTER 19

Biometric Risks Related to Identities

A few years back, biometric data from the US Office of Personnel Management (OPM) was stolen in a much publicized breach event. Unlike accounts, usernames, and credentials, this biometric data cannot be changed and is permanently linked back to an identity. For this reason, the safety of biometric data is an important consideration.

Multiple techniques are available for taking digital biometric information and creating attack tools like fake fingerprints. These are used to bypass biometric scanners or even falsify traditional paper-based applications that use ink-fingerprint techniques.

Although many vendors seem to regard biometrics as a holy grail for authentication, large-scale breaches of biometric data and the inability to rest its source highlight a flaw in this approach. For these reasons, biometric data should only be applied for authorization – never for authentication alone.

As we reviewed early, authorization, in the simplest terms, is the permission to perform a task. It is the ability to proceed without verifying who you are or who you say you are. The most common form of biometric authorization used today is Apple Pay. When placing your finger on the touch identification sensor, you are authorizing payment.

Authentication, however, is the verification of you as a person and who you say you are. It does not authorize you to perform any tasks; it just proves your identity. Authentication is primarily performed today by usernames and passwords, two-factor authentication, smart cards, and other techniques like one-time passwords. They generally tie secret knowledge to a second physical media or to the creation of a unique code of which only you have knowledge. The various components of an authentication system are designed to prove your identity, but they do not authorize you as a person to anything.

© Morey J. Haber, Darran Rolls 2020
M. J. Haber and D. Rolls, *Identity Attack Vectors*, https://doi.org/10.1007/978-1-4842-5165-2_19

So, here is where the problem lies. Some biometric technologies are blurring the line between authorization and authentication. They are taking a sophisticated approach based on technology to identify an individual (authentication) and are now merging it with the permissions to perform a task (authorization). When biometric data is compromised, security will suffer and subsequently be used to infiltrate either the user's identity or the ability to perform tasks.

Although OPM is the first major breach of this type, it does have far-reaching ramifications. The biometric data stolen can be used to craft authorization and authentication attacks against anyone breached, including some of the highest valued personas and assets in the world. Either type of attack would easily and completely bypass traditional username and password paradigms if biometrics alone is used for both. This is why there needs to be a separation between authentication and authorization and why the definitions between the two need to be clearly understood.

Biometric data is like any other form of data – it gets stored electronically. This biometric data is usually encrypted, and various forms of key mechanisms are used to ensure that one data source alone cannot reveal its contents. Vendors claim biometric data is not hack-able, but history has shown us, from the Enigma machine to the weaknesses uncovered in RSA Keys, every type of encryption can be, and will be, compromised. It is just a matter of time, persistence, and a computational speed that prevent this from happening.

While there are systems that can validly claim to be impossible to hack TODAY, that claim only has a finite lifetime. Biometric identities are stuck with you for a literal lifetime. You cannot change your fingerprints or the blood vessels in your eyes. So, by the time we are old(er), there is a good chance that the system securing our biometric data will have been compromised. Considering that we have computers from the 1950s still running air traffic flight control, power plants, and other infrastructure, it is reasonable to assume that some of today's systems and databases may also be around in 60 years' time – a sobering thought!

There is one final discussion point that's worth noting: The debate regarding biometrics is not new. The ability to steal someone's likeness is not limited to science fiction and has been documented many times in Internet memes and on TV shows like *MythBusters*. What is new is the extent that hardware and software vendors are adopting biometrics as the next-generation of security solutions.

In the last 10 years, we have seen fingerprint readers on laptops (most of which have been cracked) and facial recognition software that uses local cameras to verify user identities as part of a login prompt. In fact, most Android phones suffer from these flaws, and it has been proven that 3D printed masks (heads) can trick these systems. This next-generation push of biometrics applies multiple techniques for facial recognition (visual, infrared, etc.) and ultimately stores the data electronically, just like every previous technology has done. These devices are still computers with storage devices – encrypted or not – and biometric information needs to be retrieved somehow to complete the authentication process. Therefore, somehow, sometime, someway it will be compromised. A threat actor just needs to find that inevitable "weak link" in order to implement a successful attack vector.

The OPM breach has shown it is possible to steal biometric data. Consumers and businesses adopting biometrics need to be mindful of implementing separation of tasks and to protect accordingly. The explosion of biometric technology is not far off if we continue to blur the lines of authorization and authentications. As long as we can keep the two separate and distinct, the risk can be managed, and the future resultant predictions of identity chaos can be avoided.

CHAPTER 20

Blockchain and Identity Management

The level of hype around Bitcoin, Blockchain, and cryptocurrency is astonishing despite them still being in their infancy. When you hear your Uber driver candidly discussing it, or your local news carries a piece on how a family paid for their daughter's wedding with Bitcoin, then you know that the hype is out of control.

If you know anything about these technologies, excellent; you are ahead of the curve. Hopefully, you have not realized too late that they actually have a more limited place in business than the hype would lead us all to believe.

Understanding Blockchains and Distributed Ledger Technology

A Blockchain is simply a distributed electronic ledger system that maintains multiple copies on multiple nodes. Blockchains are not a database replacement technology, they are simply a specialized computing technique that secures data entries based on a distributed system of cryptographic verification. Blockchain itself is a specific implementation of a class of technology that is often referred to as Distributed Ledger Technology (DLT).

To truly understand how blockchain and DLT systems work, you have to understand how cryptographic hashing is used to create blocks and chains; you must also understand the notion of distributed consensus, and in the case of the Bitcoin implementation, you have to understand the principles of proof of work (see Figure 20-1).

© Morey J. Haber, Darran Rolls 2020
M. J. Haber and D. Rolls, *Identity Attack Vectors*, https://doi.org/10.1007/978-1-4842-5165-2_20

Figure 20-1. *Understanding Distributed Ledger Technology and the Blockchain*

Hashing

A cryptographic hash is a mathematical algorithm for one-way encryption that is used to create tamper-proof on-line data. The crypto hash is at the center of everything relating to Blockchain, so it is important to have at least a rudimentary understanding of how it functions.

A hash is a mathematical function that, when applied to some input data, creates a unique random digest or fingerprint, as its output (see Figure 20-2). It provides a one-way encryption process that is very costly to brute force and yet is very fast to validate. This unique property allows for the reliable tamper-proofing of the input data, without sharing that input data with a third party. If I hash something and share with you both the encrypted data and its hash value, together, we can achieve something that is often referred to as "verification without disclosure." This ability to verify the integrity of something, without sharing it, is key to how Blockchain-related systems work.

SHA256 ("HelloWorld") = Digest

Figure 20-2. *The process of cryptographic hashing*

Blocks and Chains

Hashes are used to fingerprint and verify "blocks" of data. A block consists of some header information and a payload; the payload would be the data we planned to share, plus its hash value. Each block of data is chained back to the previous block, by including its hash. So, in the example shown in Figure 20-3, the hash of Block A is included in Block B and Block B's hash is a verification of them both. Bitcoin blocks also contain ordering, time-stamping, and other important information, but this is basically how the system works. Interestingly, if you want to see live blocks on the Bitcoin Blockchain, the web site `www.blockexplorer.com` shows you this detail in the live running system.

But the really important thing about blocks is the fact that they live in a chain, with the structure and integrity of that chain provided by capturing the hash of the previous blocks. Should a malicious actor tamper with one of the blocks in the chain, it would invalidate that block's hash and as Fleetwood Mac famously put it "break the chain." The question then becomes, what stops a well-funded adversary from tampering with a block, and re calculating all the hashes that come after – something that would be computationally tiresome, but certainly very doable. The answer is something called distributed consensus.

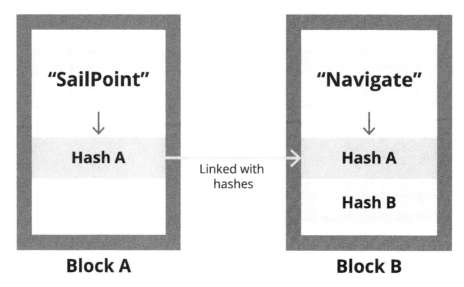

Figure 20-3. *Blocks of data in a chain*

Distributed Consensus

Distributed consensus is a very interesting concept and is one of the truly innovative elements of how DLT works. First, you have to understand that there are multiple copies of the chain, each hosted by a separate node in the network. This is called distribution and is depicted in Figure 20-4. In the case of the Blockchain, it means literally thousands of nodes all maintaining an individual copy of the chain.

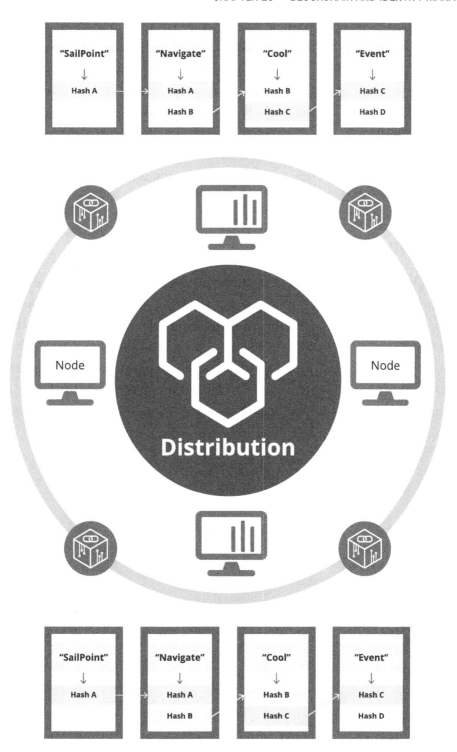

Figure 20-4. *Distributed consensus by multiple nodes hosting and publishing the chain*

Each node in the Blockchain network is busy listening for transactions (payments), creating new blocks, and competing to be the first to publish that block to the rest of the network. And when a node wins that race and does publish a block first, it must also pass validation by the rest of network participants. Unless a majority of the nodes confirm the cryptographic integrity of the chain, the newly published block is not actually accepted. Every node is, in effect, competing in a giant crypto processing race, with the express goal of being the first. This is the heart of how distributed consensus works. Literally, thousands of independent entities agree on the cryptographic integrity of the Blockchain.

Proof of Work

Nodes don't just get to publish a block without concern; they first have to solve a cryptographic puzzle to go with it. This puzzle is called a Proof of Work. In essence, a Blockchain Proof of Work is an ingenious crypto guessing game, one that involves taking a block, adding some data to the end of it – a "nonce," basically some meaningless text – and then generating a hash of the whole thing. This process is repeated again and again, until a specific numerical pattern is found in the randomness of the output. For the Bitcoin network, this is a series of preceding zeros. This is summarized in Figure 20-5.

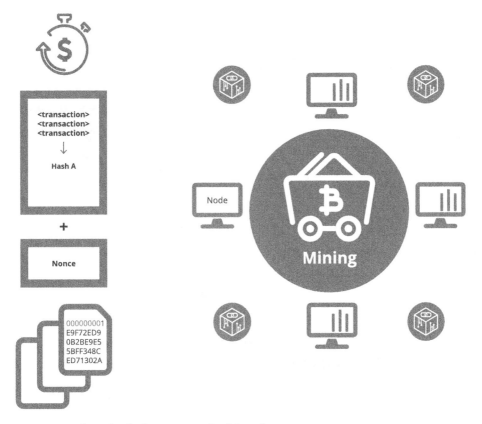

Figure 20-5. *The Blockchain Proof-of-Work system*

Realistically this process of adding data, generating a hash, and looking for training zero data is a giant game of chance. It might take hundreds of millions of guesses before the right format output is randomly generated. This computational guessing game costs time and money. To be precise, it takes about 10 minutes to solve this puzzle on one of the largest dedicated server farms in the world. So of course, this computational exercise burns CPU cycles, which consumes electricity, which costs real money. And so as soon as a node does solve this puzzle, it quickly sends off its block for validation by the rest of the network. Remember, Blockchain is a first to file AND validate paradigm.

But, if a newly published block fails validation with the majority of the nodes in the network – remember its distributed consensus – the block gets ignored, and the publisher has wasted their investment in time and money to generate it. This process of puzzle-solving and publishing of blocks is of course called crypto mining.

Now you'd be right to ask yourself, "Why do miners compete – why do they invest the time and money in a giant crypto lottery in the first place?" The answers are simple; they get paid in Bitcoin if they win. You might also ask, "Why does the Blockchain system need miners – why set the puzzle and pay the price?" The answer is that for Blockchain to work, it needs a community of participants. It needs multiple nodes hosting the chain, publishing blocks, and validating its integrity. For a system without a centralized authority to succeed, it needs to promote participation, in order to generate that much needed distributed consensus.

Pitfalls and Protections

Natively, blockchain technology associated with bitcoins can only process a limited number of transactions per second and cannot store complex records or blobs – only ledger-style information that has a finite start date, like shipping information, or inception and process dates.

This limitation has been overcome in recent iterations of blockchain that use hybrid data models or ledger-style indexes to retrieve more complex datasets. These pointers need to have access to additional datasets that may reside in another location and be secured with additional privileges. Therefore, additional files, pictures, videos, and other large datasets are just not a good fit for blockchain technology without additional storage. This is one of the problems everyone needs to understand. Think of a blockchain implementation like old school peer-to-peer (P2P) network technology from Napster, LimeWire, or BearShare. Each node contains a database of all records – any new entries need to propagate to all other nodes for validity. The difference is the data, once inserted in the ledger, is permanent and the ledger is replicated to all nodes, in its entirety, in order for resilience and integrity. Thus, the more nodes and the bigger the ledger, the slower the entire process becomes.

While a peer-to-peer network queries its peers for entries, a DLT blockchain actually contains a duplicate of all entries in relation to its peers. This means tampering with one node does not invalidate the entire blockchain. Any new entry into the blockchain has to be properly validated (via proof-of-work in the case of bitcoins) to be accepted as a ledger entry and propagated to other nodes. This is where security comes into play.

Entries into the blockchain ledger needed to be validated for fraudulent activity, and more importantly, the hosts containing blockchain implementations must be secured against vulnerabilities and privileged attacks that could compromise or tamper with blockchain insertions.

Blockchain implementations can have nodes that are explicitly trusted (usually only in commercial implementations) or out on the public Internet (like Bitcoin) where the ledger could be anywhere at any time. To that end, there is no concept of blockchain ledger modifications (entry deletion or modification). This is key to protect the integrity of the data. Once an entry is accepted by a majority of the nodes, it is considered permanent. Therefore, if you can attack the server, application, and ledger processes, you can tamper with the blockchain with fraudulent insertions. This is how some of the recent cryptocurrency attacks have been occurring. The server and application have been the target, not the blockchain directly.

Blockchain implementations are only as secure as the applications that use them. Poor security controls for inserting data in the ledger will lead to tampering. In the case of bitcoins, beyond a 51% ownership of all Bitcoin servers, the servers themselves validate their entries via a system called proof of work. Proof of work is a repeated mathematical computation designed to deter malicious actors from publishing fraudulent ledger entries.

Applying Identities to DLT

So, how do we secure blockchain implementations? We first start with basic cybersecurity hygiene. Since the ledger and its supporting infrastructure operate on a computer just like any other application, consider the following basic best practices:

- Use Identity and Access Management tools and practices to control any access to the solution or its infrastructure.

- Embrace Privileged Access Management controls for all privileged accounts related to the system and it's supporting infrastructure and ensure the host is monitored and properly managed for asset based vulnerabilities.

- Use vulnerability management software to secure the integrity of the host and applications from tampering that could lead to inappropriate read or write of blockchain ledger entries.

- Use patch management and software version management best practices for prompt remediation, mitigation, or hardening of all parts of the system.

Once the basics are covered, we need to consider the unique characteristics of a DLT implementation and protect them too:

- New entries written into the blockchain should be secured with dynamic privileges and only valid for one-time usage. This can be done with privileged password access solutions and managed keys/passwords for any API access. An insecure insertion path into the blockchain can lead to devastating results

- Reads from the blockchain should be secured in a similar fashion to ensure the retrieval is not tampered with (i.e., via a man in the middle attack) before processing by the application.

Since modifications and deletions of blockchain records are not permitted, all entries should be double-checked and verified before being written to avoid the entire model (ledger) being compromised. Think of blockchains as just another application for data storage. If your application or host can be tampered with at an account or identity level, so can your blockchain. The goal should be security and integrity best practices during both design and implementation so this can never occur.

To begin securing a blockchain, architects and security professionals must assume that the logic of the application control model approved an entry into the blockchain. This integrity check is totally the responsibility of the application using the blockchain as the data being stored could be anything from a Bitcoin transaction to manufacturing or shipping application data. Remember, once an entry is made, it cannot be deleted, modified, or suppressed, just linked with a new entry that supersedes it. This makes blockchains most suited to "new" information and not to the storage of complex changing datasets.

The question then becomes how to secure that entry so that no malicious activity can occur outside of the business logic itself. Let's start with this basic diagram and simplified workflow shown in Figure 20-6.

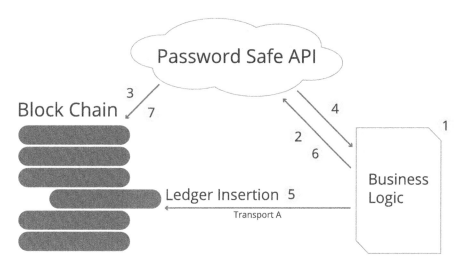

Figure 20-6. *Simplified Blockchain workflow*

1. The application's business logic approves an entry into the blockchain. Without any additional Identity Governance or PAM protections, the entry would occur through transport A and potentially could be tampered with since no additional validation is present.

2. The business logic of the application instead requests a one-time password or key from the PAM solution using a just-in-time model. This credential is valid for only one transaction (insertion or read) and can have additional access control parameters specified:

   a. Source of blockchain ledger entry

   b. Time to live

   c. Linkage to external logging or other applications

3. The privileged password management solution then sets a one-time password or key in the blockchain application which gives it permissions to write into the ledger. This could be a privileged user with write permissions, but its password or key is managed by the password safe itself. Once it is used, it is reset or invalidated.

4. The key or password, once set for the blockchain user, is then sent back to the business logic.

5. The business logic then uses transport A with the one-time credentials to insert the ledger entry.

6. Once complete, the business logic informs the password safe that the task is complete and that the one-time password should be terminated.

7. The password safe then resets the user's writeable account to a scrambled and unusable password or key by any other application to prevent rogue entries. Only the business logic can securely request a valid key or password for the next valid transaction.

While this workflow assumes a high level of confidence in business logic and a tamper-free application, it does prevent a threat actor from maliciously reading and writing to a blockchain. Since blockchains are inherently a low-volume storage medium, you would only expect a lower rate of transactions per second, resulting in less time-critical process requirements – hence nothing like the millions of transactions a second you would expect from an enterprise database.

The security of the application workflow is, therefore, managed in two parts – the business logic to approve an entry and the password safe technology to provide authentication prior to adding a new entry. Both requirements must be satisfied for a write (or possible even a read if working with extremely sensitive data) to secure the contents of the ledger. As the business community begins embracing blockchain technology, security should be a paramount concern.

Basic cybersecurity hygiene for identity access management, privileged access management, and password management can help make implementations secure above and beyond traditional database implementations. The "no-update" nature of the chaining paradigm means greater care should be taken of what gets stored. As soon as something has been committed to the ledger, it persistent for perpetuity, so greater care it required. This twist on storage approach means securing your blockchain implementation is different than anything we have implemented in the past. It requires an increased focus on identity and account best practices and not just the inherent integrity of a blockchain technology.

For all the reasons stated in the preceding text, we do not recommend using a basic blockchain to store account and identity information as a part of an extended Identity Governance process model. Instead, look to use permission controlled DLT offerings that overlay strong access controls and audit capabilities. These extended enterprise-class DLT stacks are a much better fit for systems where a centralized audit and access control model is required.

Governing Blockchain

As blockchain and enterprise-class Distributed Ledger Technology continues to gain traction, and as enterprise systems make use of the technology, it will be our job in Identity Management to help secure it. In practice, this will mean providing controls and oversight for permissioned ledgers.

So far, permissioned ledger systems seem to be trending toward a very traditional Access Control List (ACL) approach. This means that all access to the DLT system is controlled via an established account and entitlement implementation. These systems have accounts that must be created and deleted and use very normal "permission and entitlement assignment" models. For most Identity Governance systems, integrating with these systems simply means delivering a new connector that leverages the APIs provided by the permissioned ledger framework. With a basic connector in hand, the IG system is then able to manage this new resource just like any other, providing visibility, controls, and governance for its assignment lifecycle.

CHAPTER 21

Conclusion

Identity attacks cannot be prevented or solved with any single technology, tool, or technique. There is no pinch-hit quick solution. Identity and access management is an ongoing process that invariably must become a critical part of how you manage security for your infrastructure. Best practice IAM must be adopted as a part of the company culture and comprehensively implemented as part of a continuous management approach to the multiple changes, threats, and risks within your environment. In practice, this is a process that never stops since your business never stops.

As the CTO of SailPoint and the CTO and CISO of BeyondTrust, we both agree that we have the best jobs in the world! We have often had a friendly debate about which company is better to work for, but always concluded that every day we get to engage with great customers, partners, and prospects and to work with some of the smartest people in the industry. We have both found that the people we get to hang out with, like us, have a passion for identity and privilege management. Given our roles as technology innovators and advocates, we get to think deeply about and openly discuss a wide variety of security-related topics with this learned and stimulating group of people. One of the most prevalent questions we get asked is, "What is the future of identity and privilege?" With cloud, mobile, DevOps, IoT, and AI technologies now being deployed in most businesses, it's fascinating to consider where our industry will be in 10 years from now.

Sadly, neither of us have that mythical crystal ball, so predicting what challenges lie ahead in this space will always be a gamble. The best recommendation we can give is to focus on the core tenets of IAM that have been proven to work time and time again. We can advise that you should adopt and implement the security best practices that have passed the test of time (R2D2 and quantum computing aside). So, as we look back on what we've learned in this industry so far, we offer a series of what can best be described as "basic success patterns for Identity Governance and privilege management." We will, of course, continue to mature and develop our own thinking in this area, but for now at least we can offer a unified and complementary strategy for how your organization should approach our areas of expertise in governance and privilege management.

© Morey J. Haber, Darran Rolls 2020
M. J. Haber and D. Rolls, *Identity Attack Vectors*, https://doi.org/10.1007/978-1-4842-5165-2_21

For the conclusion of this book, we offer the following critical tenets of identity attack vectors and how identity access management should be embraced to make your implementation successful and stand the test of time:

1. **Think Identity and Not Account**

   Even before the advent of cloud computing, we learned that more often than not, an end user in the organization typically has multiple accounts and multiple entitlements per account across the infrastructure. If an enterprise only focuses its IAM program on managing at the account level, it will never get the total visibility needed to properly know "who does have access to what." Understanding the three-way relationship between an identity and its accounts, between the account and its entitlement, and between the entitlement and the data/information that it protects is key. By centralizing data around an identity, enterprises have a single place to model roles, policies, privileges, and risk, a single place to build out compliance/audit policies, and a unified approach to provisioning, privilege management, and access control across the organization.

2. **Visibility Is King! Silos Are Bad!**

   With new technologies like cloud, mobile, DevOps, and IoT being mixed with established enterprise mainstays like SAP, Oracle, and RACF (yes, RACF is still out there folks), everyone needs a central point of visibility. All enterprise applications that contain valuable or sensitive data or any process that performs mission-critical IT operations must be managed with a focus on automation, governance, and compliance. This single point of visibility allows the organization to leverage common detective and preventative controls and to ensure an enterprise-wide view of its identity and access data. This enables the business and IT to effectively analyze risk, make informed decisions, and implement appropriate controls in an automated and sustainable fashion.

3. **Full Lifecycle Identity Governance Is a Requirement**

   It is critical to always manage the lifecycle of an identity and its access by tying it to the business policies and business owners that are responsible for it. We must allow best practice Identity Governance policies to span the entire lifecycle of an identity – from joiners to movers and leavers and throughout the processes of access request, provisioning, and access review. By embedding policies and controls throughout the full identity lifecycle process, organizations can achieve enhanced automation, sustainable compliance, and reduced security risk.

4. **Deploy Integrated Privileged Access Management**

   With the focus of the adversary clearly directed to the compromise of privileged access in applications and infrastructure, it is essential that you take a comprehensive and integrated approach to the vaulting, auditing, and monitoring of privileged credentials and access. This means a lot more than choosing the right PAM vendor and the best tooling; it means comprehensively integrating that technology with your wider security ecosystem. Specifically, integrating PAM and Identity Governance should be a "must have," and providing audit, controls, and governance for the composition, assignment, and usage of the PAM infrastructure is of paramount importance.

5. **Adopt a Predictive Approach**

   Machine learning and artificial intelligence technology is being embraced by vendors and businesses alike. You should look to leverage this important new technology to help security staff, compliance teams, and the broader business user community make smarter and more informed access decisions. Specifically look for knowledge, insights, and recommendations to be fully integrated with your Identity Governance process flows, delivering more real-time policies, better access certification decision, smarter controls, and more informed governance.

6. **Implement Least Privilege**

   With accounts and entitlements under constant attack, it
   becomes increasingly critical that we continue to drive toward
   a least privilege approach to access. This means making more
   informed and more fine-grained access decisions, both close to
   the actual access decision and back out at the time of assignment,
   provisioning, and lifecycle management. In practice, it also means
   designing smaller and more granular password vaults, designing
   more fine-grained entitlements, and the adoption of a more agile
   and responsive approach to the assignment and removal of access
   wherever it resides.

7. **The User Experience Is Everything!**

   Identity governance and privilege management technology must
   help provide a better overall user experience. Having the right
   business user experience for these critical security processes is an
   essential part of achieving widespread participation and adoption
   within your organization. The usage experience of these tools
   and techniques must feel part of the business flow, rather than a
   separate, "tacked-on" process.

Index

© Morey J. Haber, Darran Rolls 2020
M. J. Haber and D. Rolls, *Identity Attack Vectors*, https://doi.org/10.1007/978-1-4842-5165-2

Made in the USA
Coppell, TX
18 May 2023